'JUL 4 2000

D0818894

Secre
Success

Expanded Second Edition

Secrets of the Successful Student

The best selling guide to the Real Stuff of campus life

Gordon D. Stein

With cover & drawings by Peter M. Herman
a.k.a. Carbo of the Flying Caborski Brothers
Additional drawings by Iryna Molodecky

Culture Concepts

Secrets of the Successful Student
Second Expanded Edition
Copyright © 1991, 1994 Gordon D. Stein

ISBN 0-921472-20-X

First edition, 1991
Second expanded edition, 1994

Canadian Cataloguing in Publication Data
Stein, Gordon D. (Gordon David), 1961-
Secrets of the successful student
Expanded 2nd ed.
ISBN 0-921472-20-X
1. College student orientation. 2. College students – Life skills guides.
3. College students – time management. 4. Study skills. I. Title
LB2343.3.S74 1994   378.1'98   C94-931969-4

Culture Concepts books are available at special discounts for
bulk purchases as premiums, or for fund-raising, sales promotions
or educational use. Please contact us at:
CULTURE CONCEPTS INC.
5 Darlingbrook Crescent
Toronto Ontario Canada M9A 3H4
Telephone 416-231-1692
Fax: 416-237-1832

Illustrations by Peter M. Herman and Iryna Molodecky
Design by Robert MacDonald

Printed and bound in Canada

About the author

Gord Stein won the Procter & Gamble Engineering Award during his degree in Mechanical Engineering at The University of Western Ontario, was on the Dean's List twice during his studies for Master of Business Administration at the University of Toronto and successfully completed the Canadian Securities Course.

But it was the shock of a 20% midterm in first year engineering that spurred his interest in just what it takes to be a successful student, and how to help other students make it through.

He did complete that engineering degree and has worked in a variety of roles in Engineering, Systems Analysis, Sales and Marketing, and Management. An avid fitness enthusiast, Gord enjoys sailboat racing, wind surfing and running, and he has completed the New York City Marathon and the Toronto Marathon.

He lives in Toronto with his wife Ingrid and son Connor.

Acknowledgments

Thanks to all who helped me to discover and to let out The Secrets. Especially my two illustrators, "Carbo Caborsky" and Iryna Molodecky. Also thanks to Karisa Ambury, Cindy Faber, Cheryl Watson, Mark Kindrachuk and his personal computer, as well as a tough but superb editor at Culture Concepts.

And for this second edition, thanks to the teachers, the principals, the instructors, the professors and the countless students across the country who took the time to share their ideas and recipes with me.

And most of all a special thanks to my wife Ingrid who smiled endlessly but reassuringly through my hundreds of whaddayathinks. And to Connor who laughs at everything I do.

DEDICATION

To my mother
who made me a writer
and to my wife
who made me write.

Contents

Fore Words

PART ONE:
HERE'S LOOKING AT YOU

Chapter 1:
Your Student Hovel
A primer on cockroaches, mice and leaks.

Chapter 2:
Fiscal Frenzy
Tackling the cash flow challenge

Chapter 3:
Beyond the Care Package
Cooking and eating cheap and good

Chapter 4:
Fighting Student Stress and Spread
Workin' it all out

Chapter 5:
Examining the Student Body
Steps to dynamic dating

PART TWO:
LET'S GET SERIOUS

Chapter 6:
Post Procrastinating
Time management for the rushin' student

Chapter 7:
Organized Grime
Papers, laundry and cupboards

Chapter 8:
Avoiding Arithmetic Armageddon
Breaking the math barrier

Chapter 9:
The Taming of the Verb
Essays and research made easy

Chapter 10:
Making the Grade
You too can pass exams

Chapter 11:
Creating a Career
Post grad proving ground

After Words

Fore Words

Looking for a student study guide crammed with useful formulae, handy math tables, summaries of the great works of literature and some speed reading tips?

Keep looking.

On to the REAL STUFF of campus life.

How do you find a decent place to live? And if it turns out to be not so decent, what do you do about the calamities that are now part of your life? How do you make sure that you won't run out of money three months into the year? What to do about the hunger pangs and lack of basic know-how in the kitchen department? How about some student chow that anyone can cook fast, on the cheap and happens to be good for you too?

How do you ease the stress and tighten the spreading waist line? How do you expand the hours and keep those shuffling notes in some kind of order? How to handle the math blues and solve the essay mysteries? How to handle exam day?

And after graduation, what?

Welcome to *Secrets of the Successful Student: The best selling guide to the Real Stuff of campus life.*
Here's a stick of dynamite that will propel you through the labyrinths of higher learning and blast you out on

graduation day with great marks, a full social calendar, a balanced cheque book and even a great body.

Along the way, you'll learn to cook some Lemon, Lime and Lager Chicken (a fought-after secret recipe), find the best places to spark a new romance and how to control both the mice and the roommates in your apartment.

Never before have all of these really critical matters been laid out so clearly for the new college or university student, referenced so succinctly for the currently enrolled (there's always something more to learn) or has such a briskly delightful stroll through memory lane for the paunchy, greying sophomore of yesteryear ever been bound in a book.

Everything that you'll need to get through those campus years is in these pages. Except of course, a chapter on cleaning.

After all, we're students aren't we?

Gord Stein

PART ONE

=

HERE'S LOOKING AT YOU

=

Chapter 1: Your Student Hovel
A primer on cockroaches, mice and leaks

Chapter 2: Fiscal Frenzy
Tackling the cash flow challenge

Chapter 3: Beyond the Care package
Cooking and eating cheap and good

Chapter 4: Fighting Student Stress and Spread
Workin' it all out

Chapter 5: Examining the Student Body
Steps to dynamic dating

=

Your Student Hovel

=

A primer on cockroaches, mice and leaks

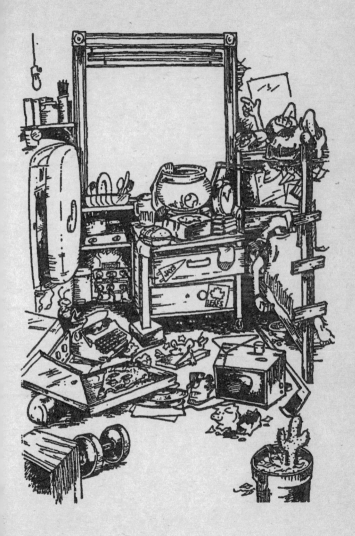

You have just read the same paragraph in your Geography text for the seventh time. Enough. You saunter over to the couch to take a study break, ease the aching shoulders, and watch some Flintstones reruns.

HOLY $*%^$&!@$%$%^!

A broken spring on the couch pierces your jeans, stabs you in the butt and sends you streaking to your feet. A warm trickle of blood tracks its way down your thigh. As the pain subsides, you ponder the date of your last tetanus shot. Ah well, with your schedule this term, there is no time for tetanus shots anyway.

Settling back into the show – and a safer spot on the couch – you are watching as Fred fastens Wilma's rock necklace before going to the Royal Order of the Water Buffalo Gala ball, when you are suddenly aware of a scampering sound in your room. A mouse scoots in behind the...

A mouse? A moouuusse? A MOUSE!!!

Leaping to the broom closet in search of artillery, a plume of dust billows up in your wake. Where's the broom? Not surprisingly, it is occupying a lonely spot behind the more regularly used items like skis, footballs, evil smelling gym bags and a twenty pound bag of mouldy spuds.

THE BROOM, THE BROOM. Where's the B..R..OOOOM?

The final tug that sets the broom free unleashes an avalanche of additional sporting goods from the straining shelf that held it all. Oh boy. This is going to take forever to... Later.

Meanwhile, our racing rodent hero is still shadowboxing the dust bunnies lurking under the book shelf. A deft swat with the broom sends him scurrying along the baseboard, his tiny paws gaining superb traction on the sticky floor. You join the chase, stumbling over a stack of newspapers on the way to the kitchen. Where'd he go? You tensely scan the dust, the hair, and the dollops of spaghetti sauce that must have been left by the previous tenants.

Suddenly, eye contact. Glazed, wide and determined eyes lock with tiny sneering ones.

The mouse dashes under the radiator. You wind up with your broom. There's the tip of his tail by the leg of the radiator. You feel your sinews straining your skin, and a trickle of sweat drips over your eye. You see his nose and whiskers brush by the radiator valve. Fixing your eye on the target and beginning to unwind, you see the tiny claws attempt a final chin up on the pipe by the valve. As your torso twists, he turns to look, almost as if in dare. A swoosh of the broom, milliseconds to contact. The broom connects, sending the radiator valve, the mouse and a burst of water spurting wildly against the ceiling.

When the fire department arrives, explanations are difficult. Your mouth sputters only a stream of "I can't believe its" at the puddled floor, the dripping furniture, the stained sports stuff, the scattered soaked books and papers.

It seems that the tenant in the apartment below was flooded out and assumed that sprinklers had gone off upstairs. Doing her civic duty, she had contacted the fire department to investigate. One by one the neighbours, the landlord, and then a bevy of curious onlookers, all in varying states of dress and undress, gathered to savour the sight of a soul dejected, distraught and drenched.

Transfixed by the sight, the huddled onlookers stared relentlessly. Few things brighten one's spirit quite as much as the sight of someone else's stumbling stupidity. It's consoling to realise there are other losers.

You are not among the consoled.

Meanwhile, after carefully surveying the water, the pile of wet newspapers, the closet poltergeist and the curious crowds, one of the onlookers shook the water out of his fur, and silently scurried out the open door in search of cheese.

New Learning Dimensions: Housing Nightmares

While your student housing nightmares may not end up being quite this desperate, most students face some sort of housing problems during their years at school.

Erratic heating and cooling systems, building managers who don't want to hear about mice, filth, fleas, noisy and/or slovenly and/or broke roommates, cockroaches, thieves, temperamental plumbing and sporadic electricity, rent increases and leaky roofs, can all add new learning dimensions to your school years.

Stay with the folks?

First decision is whether you can stay at home with the folks during your school years. Parents can be reasonable, but let's also be realistic. They are parents, after all.

Are they going to understand when you come home covered in purple dye as a result of some orientation ritual? Can they really fall asleep to the sound of your computer keyboard clicking into the wee hours of the night? Will they be receptive to an impromptu Tequila shot party in their basement at 3 AM? When you borrow your mom's best dress for the Halloween pub and it comes back marinated in a buddy's vomit and the remnants of a chili dog, will she understand? Will she nod sagely and mutter things about how she remembers school too?

Is it any easier for women? Will you be able to bring home that long-haired, rock singer with numerous metallic items piercing through the skin on his face? What if he asks your Dad where he got his cardigan? Will your relationship come to a screeching halt if Dad monopolizes him for a three hour inspection of his workshop, only 200 of his tour group vacation slides or his trout fly collection?

If you have money, you move out. If you don't, you still move out.

Obviously, there are a number of dire consequences to be considered before entertaining the thought of living at home with your parents while going to school. Generally it boils down to simple arithmetic and geography. If you have money, you move out.

If you don't and you live near school, you stay with your folks, save the cash and develop a sudden interest in making perogies and balloon curtains with mom and installing garage door openers and watching fishing shows with dad. And figure a way to raise the cash to make that move.

Finding that Elemental Shelter

Ha! I knew you wouldn't cut it living with Mom and Dad! OK, let's find you a place to live.

As in all aspects of life, businesses will generally spring up poised to sap the cash from the uninformed, the desperate, the unfortunate, the about-to-become unfortunate and yes, even the student. I refer to those firms that specialize in locating accommodations for you, the starving student. There is absolutely no reason why you should pay someone to find you accommodations. There are a whole host of building managers and homeowners out there looking for decent tenants just like you.

All you have to do is find them and convince them of your decency.

Perils and pragmatics of residence living

Most colleges and universities have built-in accommodations called residences that provide some sort of shelter from the elements. More often than not they are equipped with running water. Some even have drains that work to carry all of this running water away. Kidding aside, residence accommodation may be the thing for you. It is cheap and often includes a deal on what could loosely be termed meals.

On the other hand, the rooms are the size of a Volkswagen trunk. The halls carry a continual stream of vocal excesses that can only come from those who are, apparently for the first time in their life, more than ten feet from their parents' grasp. For the next several months there remains a brave few who hew to the solemn proclamation that 'the whole thing will quiet down as we get further into the term'.

Residences also carry an institutional feel that is particularly disquieting. An institutional feel? Imagine living in a hospital and eating at the cafeteria, waiting to get your appendix out. Now imagine yourself staying there for three or four years.

Let me add a couple more wrinkles. You are staying there while going to school, not waiting to have your appendix out. Get the idea? I, for one, cannot feel at home hearing my heels click on white tiles passing a janitor operating one of those huge floor polishers on the way to my sterile little room amidst a battalion of Neanderthal residence dwellers. That said, it's up to you, they are cheap and livable. For a year or two. Maybe just for the first term?

Those prospective room renters

The school will, however, most likely have a housing office where prospective room renters will post listings describing their offerings. I use the term 'describing' loosely since space is often at a premium and a listing may appear something like this:

> **'Lvly thr bdrm twnhs ovrlkng lke wth
> w/o dck, stps t trnsprtn,
> bdrm whr ld, $335+, refs, frst, lst."**

This one, for example, indicates a student ghetto type of row house that overlooks another row house where one of the tenants apparently leaves his blinds open and the sports channel blaring. There is 'wiped out' deck out back that was supposed to have been rebuilt by city ordinance after a previous tenant twisted her ankle in a gopher hole. The hovel is within several thousand steps of public transportation and has no parking provisions. Broadloom is provided where laid, providing you provide and lay it.

A panel of referees will scrutinize you and if you are the first one to show any interest, they will grab you. It is recommended that you do not speak with the tenant who was there last.

So what to do?

Make up a list of the features that you would like and the features that you must have. (Laundry, public transportation, heat and hydro costs, parking etc.) Rank them in importance. On another piece of paper create a matrix with headings across the top for address, renter or building manager's name, phone, rent and features. As you go through the listings posted at the housing office, jot down the addresses, the names and the phone numbers of the ones that look interesting.

Find yourself a phone and call each, asking about the features and, if you are interested, when you can come to view the premises. If, for some reason, you couldn't get through, be sure to write down the reason: busy signal, renter out, answering machine or someone else waiting for the pay phone who made you feel so guilty that you just couldn't make the last call or two.

The local newspapers are also a good source of housing opportunities with the one caveat that they may not be willing to rent to students. In most locales, this is contrary to human rights legislation, but try finding a lawyer who will fight it for free. That is if it's a place you really want and you have the time or the urge to fight.

And when?

Back to the newspaper ads. The best time to tackle them is early on a Saturday morning and weeks before classes start. Most of the ads have just come out for the first time and you will have a chance to beat the thundering herds of students and apartment hunters that form your competition. You will get first crack at the pristine suites with a view of the beach below, the ocean breaking on the rocks, while you sip the bubbly in the salon, idly glancing at a text book.

If nothing else, hopefully you will find a place with stains in the toilet bowl that can be removed without toxic chemicals and power tools.

Meeting the prospective landlady or landlord

OK. I know the scene. You are a student right? You want to be comfortable, you want to look cool. If you are a guy, you got the rips in the jeans, drip of mustard stain on the sweatshirt, little pierced hole in the nose with a chain hangin' out of it, no problems. If you are a gal, you got the black tights and the oversized sweatshirt and the fifties earrings, hey that's OK too. No problems. I hear you.

There's no need for the argyle socks and the bow tie for the guys but you might want to spruce up your look just a little before you head out to meet your prospective new landlord or landlady. It's like anything else in life, sometimes you have to look the part that you aren't. And if a clean pair of jeans and a nice shirt is what it takes to land you the new pad that will make you the envy of your class, what the hell.

And it's ditto for the gals. Just wear some dark glasses so that no one recognizes you.

What to Look For: The Obvious and the Obscure

The sniff test and other basics

As you work your way through potential dwellings, look not only for the obvious, but for the subtle and even all but obscure clues.

Begin by taking a good whiff of the place. Damp? Mildew? Just because the place smells like the inside of a sailboat is no indication that you are headed for a spot on "Lifestyles of the Rich and Famous." It is virtually impossible to get rid of that odour which will eventually permeate everything that you own, including your stereo, your goldfish and your chemistry notes.

There is also a reason why the smell is there to begin with. Check for water stains along the baseboards, on the ceilings or on the carpets, especially in basement locales. Any signs of dampness? Move on. Unless you crave green and yellow mould on your shoes.

So the place seems reasonably dry and as you amble through checking out the details, you notice that the couple who came in after you seem to be quite keen. The place seems decent, but what if they grab it before you do? If they did, you might not be able to find another one as nice. What if this is the last decent apartment in the city? Maybe you should just get out your cheque book...

Hold it! Be honest. Was that you, mentally calculating the total of first and last month's rent? For shame. You haven't finished inspecting yet!

Open some cupboards in the kitchen. Any signs of mouse traps, roach motels, chemical warfare gear or fly paper? Yech. It's enough of a jungle out there without having to fight the local wildlife for food from your own kitchen.

Are the faucets leaking? If the faucets are leaking, how good is the owner going to be about getting some heat going for you in February before you die of exposure? Is there adequate cupboard space in the off chance that a relative dies and bequeaths groceries to you? Is there room in the closet for the real necessities like sports equipment, bulky jackets and sweaters and the vacuum cleaner from the garage sale?

Testing water consuming activities

Lets check out the bathroom. If there is going to be more than one of you living there, water pressure is going to be important. With two showers going, a load of laundry in and the kitchen tap leaking, someone is going to flush a toilet and leave your soap-encrusted body to dry out in the shower for hours until someone else ends their water consuming activity. All common enough in older houses and decaying buildings.

To test the water pressure, try running the tap in the sink, start the shower and then flush the toilet. Still some water flowing in the shower? You are probably OK. Water go to a trickle or nothing at all? Could be problems.

While you are in there, check for mildew. Mildew is the black, evil smelling, gooey stuff that tends to congregate in bathrooms between the tiles, or where the tiles meet the edge of the tub. In advanced stages, it can develop into moss or even lichens. Not collectible, though.

At this point, it's your call. If it grew before, it might grow again. If it has advanced to the stage where you actually have small mushrooms sprouting from the grout, you should find yourself another place. What if your date saw such a bathroom? Besides, mother would be appalled.

Checking furniture, closets and such

With minimal vegetation in the bathroom, you can consider the bedroom. Is there ample room for your desk, bed and furniture? Can you hang more than two T shirts in the closet? Any signs of water damage on the ceiling that might indicate a leaky roof?

Back to the closet for your now-routine check for mouse traps, roach motels, chemical warfare gear and fly paper. Not to discriminate against other life forms. Some people don't seem to mind shared accommodation even when they thought they had the place to themselves. Still, nice to know what you are getting into ahead of time.

Scanning other amenities

So far so good? Great. Now its time to check out the amenities. Is there a nice backyard with a deck on which to sip cool ones and uh, er, study? If you are lucky enough to afford a car, is there a place to park the heap? Does it cost extra? Where is the nearest bus? How about laundry?

Do some careful listening

Consider what the neighbours and the neighbourhood is like. If the place is in one of those high rise apartment buildings, you might want to hang out for a bit and do some careful listening. If it seems that there are divorce proceedings under way in the apartment to the North, kids training for some sort of Bruce Lee remake to the South, Rock 'N Roll deadheads with stereos blaring to the West and some sort of amateur musician torturing his clarinet to the East, it may be time to consider other accommodations.

Be sure to do your listening on a Sunday afternoon when everyone is home and noise levels are likely to be at a peak.

And Then There Are High-Rise Alternatives

Don't forget to consider alternatives beyond the high rise apartment building. Sometimes part of a duplexed house can provide a very decent lifestyle. Find one in a nice neighbourhood with reasonable people living in the other half, some reasonable house mates for your half and you are all set.

If you live in one of those cosmopolitan cities with a heavy urban renewal program, you might even be able to get a deal on a converted warehouse and get some sort of hi-tech urban thing happening. Sometimes you might luck into a whole house that could be shared.

Also, check which bills you will be responsible for and figure that into your affordability calculations. If you live in a cold locale and the place is heated by electricity, and you have to pay the bills, you may have big problems. You will either freeze to death or you will need some sort of incredible part time job, in say, risk arbitrage to pay the bills. Make sure all roommates have signed one lease, so that if one moves out, you are not stuck with the financial responsibility. But more about legalities later.

The cave experience...

Anything goes.

I recall living in a place we called The Cave. The owner was a friend of my roommate-to-be. He was a sax player in a bar band and owned a tiny house with an unfinished basement. In May, (like a total buffoon) I agreed to rent what looked like the cave they bricked Fortunato into as he cried out for mercy. According to the sax player-landlord-carpenter, while it didn't look like much now, by August, he promised that the mirrored tiles would pick up the streaming sunlight from the new windows and gently dust it onto the granite columns...

Returning in August from a summer job out of town, I found essentially the same dark, dusty basement that I had viewed in May. A cascade of assurances were buttressed with a tide of promises, but very little construction. In the end, I pitched in and did much of the drywall, wiring, plumbing and flooring. As the November snow began to fly, I even had an entrance door to cover the gaping hole left by the jackhammer that cleared the original entrance opening back in September.

Although I lived most of that first term in a construction zone, the first couple months were free and I have since saved thousands of dollars by putting to use my desperately founded renovation skills. What the hell!

The library experience ...

Then there was the guy at my school who lived in the library.

He would slink in just before closing and hide up in the Greek Mythology book stacks. There he had cached his sleeping bag, clothing supply and a muffled alarm clock. In the morning, he would head down to the university gym for a shower and a shave and off to class with a paper cup of coffee from the cafeteria and a donut between his teeth. Your school may have motion detectors in the library to guard against this technique, but for those cash-strapped months it may be a thought...

Leases and Contracts: Avoiding Renter's Remorse or Worse

Back to finding your new place. Try to look at a few places before you commit. Few things can wrench your guts as badly as buyer's remorse. If you grab the place you are looking at right now and a friend invites you over to the spotless pad with the Jacuzzi and sun deck for which she pays $100.00 less per month, how will you feel? If you look at only two places, you can at least feel smug about the fact that some poor schlep will get stuck with that other place that you so wisely turned down.

With your mind made up, it's time to sign. Don't panic. Most landlords will use a standard form lease. In North America, in landlord Vs tenant matters the tenant generally carries the upper hand. If you are in doubt, look up the appropriate government agency that deals with tenant rights. Give them a call before you commit to anything that seems fishy. Give the lease a good read through and ask about anything that doesn't seem reasonable. Usually the deal is fairly straightforward.

Generally, the landlady will want first and last month's rent up front, so that if you skip out at any time, she has the next month's rent covered to pay the mortgage while she searches for a new tenant. Damage deposits (money paid up front to insure against potential damages) may not be legal, so check before paying one. Some owners or building managers used to prorate rent to students since they tended to skip out without paying rent through the summer months. That too, is usually illegal.

With your contract signed, its usually a matter of handing over first and last month's rent, getting the keys and voila. But here is a small final checklist:

• Make sure that you get day and nighttime phone numbers for your building manager or the house owner as well.

• Is there someone else that you can call in the case of an emergency?

• Find out how to control the heat and the air conditioning, and where's the electrical panel?

• Be sure to get receipts for your first and last month's rent and for the months in between. You might be able to claim these amounts on your income tax.

• Finally, it is imperative that you call an insurance company to get a tenant's package on your new place to protect you in case of fire, flooding or theft. The hundred bucks a year or so is worth the peace of mind since, in most cases, the landlord is not responsible should the pipes burst and soak all your goodies.

The Big Move

Before the big move

Before you move out of your parent's house be sure to squirrel away any items that they may have that would prove useful in your new abode. In particular, look for blenders (great for making a quick breakfast shake with fruit and yogurt, not to mention Margaritas and Daiquiris), kitchen items (in case you plan on eating anything during the next three years), blankets, artwork, rugs, furniture (couches made out of empty beer cases and milk crates can look a touch stark after a while) and pretty well anything else you can manage to cart away.

Most parents have a strong instinct to shower you with all manner of goodies when you leave their nest. Apparently (no pun intended) this instinct is actually a vestige from the nesting instinct that caused them to gather all the necessary gear they needed for your arrival. If your parents seem to lack this crucial reflex and simply wave goodbye, you may have to do some work to cultivate it in them before saying goodbye.

Whatever happens, do not turn anything down. Even if you can't use it or wouldn't be caught dead wearing it, you might be able to sell it to raise some cash or burn it to help keep your place cozy in the winter.

Moving Day

If you are like most students, moving should be a snap. Be careful with the stereo, throw the rest of the stuff in garbage bags, recruit a half dozen of the largest people you know (or can meet in time before the move) and presto!

To make life easier during the move, here are a few more tips: Before the move, scour local liquor and grocery stores for good boxes. Buy yourself a roll of packing tape and a heavy felt tip marker. Load the boxes with items that are destined for a common room. Seal them with your new roll of packing tape and, you guessed it, write the detailed contents and the destination room on the outside of the box with that new marker.

When your buddies come, they will know exactly where to take everything. All you have to do is bum a truck or a van from someone, buy a case of beer and order the pizza.

Problems? What Problems?

So you have been happily living in your new place for a month or two when something happens. What happens? Who knows?

It could be anything, but it is a problem if it comes up and you don't know what to do about it. First of all, don't panic. Don't worry about it either. Think of all the times that you have agonized over something and then it never happened. And even when it did it wasn't half as bad as your vivid imagination.

Best of all, these little nightmares will provide you with great material to bore your kids with thirty years from now. With a clear, relaxed mind and the handy little house problem guide that follows, you will be ready for anything. Well, OK almost anything.

Fry an egg on the window sill?

Let me guess. It is the summer, you are attending the University of Amarillo and the air conditioner that is supposed to keep the fish bowl from boiling over, isn't. A scorpion just staggered by and fainted. Apparently heat prostration. What to do?

First, determine if the place has an air conditioner. Any big grey boxes poking their nose out the window?

How about a big grey box outside somewhere with hoses that head into the house? No? Well you have no air conditioner and the building manager lied.

If you are in a hot climate and really have no air conditioning, try a little 'passive cooling.' Keep the blinds on the sunny side of the house closed during the day. Minimize cooking inside (probably the easy part) and try to live in the lower floors of the place if it has multiple levels. Get a fan or two to get some air moving. If it gets really miserable, try taking some cool showers.

If you have one of those room air conditioners, first check to ensure that it is plugged in. Next, try setting the temperature to "coldest" and turning the thing on. If it runs, but doesn't spit out cold air, the unit needs to be serviced. Call your landlord or landlady (those emergency numbers, remember?) or take the thing in to a service centre.

If you throw the switch and you get nothing, you have a blown fuse. Take a flashlight and find the fuse box for the house (a large grey metal box screwed in to the wall with a hinged door on the front). They are usually in the basement somewhere or hidden in a closet. Pull the door open and you should see a number of round glass fuses. Shine your flashlight on them. Most should look shiny and clean inside the glass, but you may have one that looks like all hell has broken loose inside.

Unscrew the little sucker and take it to a hardware store (or even a corner variety store) and ask the nice clerk for one just like it. Go for broke and get a spare one for next time. Walk your new fuse home, screw it in and try the A/C out one more time. Hopefully that should do it. Make sure nothing else is plugged in to the same circuit, or the fuse may blow again.

What's that you say? No little glass fuses? You say that you have a bunch of black switches in your grey box? Even better. Look for one of them that doesn't seem to be lined up with the rest. Flip it back and forth once to reset it and to get it to line up with the other ones. That's it.

If you have central air conditioning (big grey box outside somewhere) you will have a control for it somewhere within your apartment or house. It's a little beige box on the wall somewhere with some numbers on it. Is there a little switch on it somewhere that says "Heat Off Cool"? If it isn't switched to "Cool," it may be as simple as that. Also look for, "Fan On Auto". When the pointer is at "Fan On" that means the cool air continues to circulate. "Auto" means the fan is only going when the cooling system is on. Next, try setting the temperature to a lower setting (try 20C or 70F).

Ahh, the whoosh of cool air throughout your home. Still no luck? Best to call that emergency number again.

Cat frozen in his tracks?

Don't tell me. Let me guess. You have been reading the problems of the student at U of Amarillo and you are green with envy. Make that blue with envy. With slurred speech, blue lips, chattering teeth and your body restricting blood flow to the extremities to ensure warmth of your vital organs, you strain your numb fingers to turn these pages in search of warmth. Strain no more.

To begin, try to figure out what heats the place. Do you have large metal finned things in each of the rooms? They are radiators. With a little coaxing, we should be able to get some heat out of them. Or perhaps you have grates on the walls or floors which are supposed to spew forth warm air. They are part of a forced air system. You can't do much with these yourself other than adjust the thermostat.

Or you may have long skinny beige metal things that run along the floorboards. These are electric baseboard heaters. I will have to deal with these different types one at a time.

About radiators

OK. First you radiator people. Scoot around the place and see if your radiators are hot or warm. Are they cold? Are they all cold? If some are good and warm and some are cold, you will have to bleed any that are cold. Ah, you don't like bloodshed or you are a conscientious objector? No problem.

First, make sure that the valve at the bottom of the radiator on the pipes is open. Try turning it counter-clockwise to open it. If it was closed (all the way counter-clockwise) that might have been your problem right there.

Next, somewhere near the top of the radiator there will be a small knob. Put a glass under the knob and loosen it (counter-clockwise). It should hiss for a while. Let it hiss as long as it likes. When it is through hissing, you will see a few drops of water come out. Tighten the knob back up and the radiator (and you) will be warm shortly.

Some of these bleed valves will need to be loosened with a screwdriver. Whatever you do, be gentle so that you don't start the thing leaking.

If all your radiators are cold, or if you are one of those forced air people that I described earlier, head to the thermostat on the wall (probably a little beige box on the wall in the living or dining room). There should be a little switch on the side that says, "Heat Off Cool". Switch the thing to "Heat" and turn the setting up to 70F or 20C. Give it a minute and see if you feel any signs of warmth. If you are warm, great. Otherwise, call that number again.

About baseboard heaters

Ah, you baseboard people are still out there and shivering, aren't t t tttt ttt yyyy ooouuu? Take a look at one of those long skinny beige things attached to the wall just above the floor. Is there a round knob on it that looks like it might control the heat coming out of it? It does. Try turning it clockwise to see if it starts spitting out some heat. No luck? Call the landlord or the landlady.

No knob on the heater? Is there one on a wall in the room somewhere? Maybe hidden behind a bookcase or a plant, or lurking at the back of a drawer? If you find one, try setting it higher. If you can't find it, call the building manager. They are never around when you need them.

And then came the floods

You have woken up or come home to discover the place awash in water. Omigod. Is the water still flowing? If it is winter time, it was probably a pipe that burst. Alternatively, a sink or tub has overflowed. If so, and you know where the main water valve is (a good thing to know) for your house or apartment, go shut it off by turning the valve clockwise.

If the water is from a sprinkler system, call the fire department but only if it isn't obvious that they have already been there. Otherwise, it could be a backed up sewer or a leaky basement. Move to higher ground taking with you anything of consequence that needs to stay dry. Call the landlord or the landlady for help.

Plugged sinks?

You can brush your teeth in the sink, head off to school, get some lunch, enjoy a game of squash and make it home before the sink drains? No problem. If you are mechanically inclined, you can take apart that strange curved pipe underneath the sink (the "P trap") and clean it out. Be forewarned. Lurking within that trap is the slimiest, ugliest, stinkiest little beastie you have ever seen in your life.

Never mind Aliens and old Stephen King movies. THIS STUFF IS GROSS. Generally it is a mixture of hair, partially decomposed food, slime, goo and miscellaneous smelly black stuff.

If I have twigged your curiosity and you own a monkey wrench, read on. If you don't, how come you aren't cultivating useful friends? Get a bucket under the P trap and affix your wrench to one of the large nuts on the pipe. Loosen the nut (counter-clockwise), while bracing the pipe with your free hand. Be gentle. With the one nut loosened off, undo the other one. With the nuts taken off, pull the trap down. Ssssloosh.

Ugh. Did the trap beastie come out? I know. What a stench. I warned you. Use a screwdriver or a coat hanger to poke out the remaining sludge and then reassemble the works. Run some water and check for leaks.

Don't have the nerve, the wrench or the mechanical skill? Have a peek under the sink at the pipes. If they are old and ugly, they are cast iron. Shiny orange metal? They are copper. Black plastic? These are ABS plastic pipes. Go to the hardware store, tell 'em what kind of pipes you have and get some drain cleaner.

Be careful with this stuff. Read the directions carefully and be sure to wear whatever protective gear they recommend. Pour the stuff down the drain and flush with water as the directions outline. Still have problems? Back to the building manager.

Plugged toilets?

You've been there yourself. You are out on a heavy date with this awesome vision or dreamy hunk and you head back for a nightcap. Suddenly, you feel this tremendous urge to go to the bathroom. You politely inquire as to its whereabouts, dash in and do what you have to. Then the panic strikes.

You press the lever hoping for a powerful flush to swoosh away all of the evils that you have left there, but little happens. All the little goodies float around aimlessly in the bowl. A second flush yields few additional results. Worse, the water inside is rising and so is your pulse rate. Time ticks on. Your dreamboat calls out from the living room to see if you are OK. Now you feel the heat rise up in your cheeks...

Unplugging a toilet is not a pleasant affair, but it is generally straightforward. If it is plugged and continuing to fill up, locate the shiny chrome valve on the water inlet pipe near the wall and shut it off (clockwise). Now take a toilet plunger (if there is one tucked behind the door or somewhere) and place it over the large hole in the bowl of the toilet and give it a half dozen good thrusts. Release. Any action? Try smearing a little Vaseline around the edge of the plunger to give it a better seal, then another few good plunges. That should do it.

Keep repeating the process until it flushes properly. If you are still out of luck, you are going to have to fess up to your date. If the embarrassment is just too much, try sliding out the bathroom window. If you get a call later on, just say that you were appalled by the mess in their bathroom and you just don't think that it can work out between you.

And a few environment-friendly tips. If a plunger or a plumber's metal snake won't clear the drains, try pouring about half a mug of baking soda and half a mug of white vinegar down the drain pipe and cover with a stopper. Doesn't hurt to pour down some boiling water now and then too. Or use the soda and vinegar treatment as another prevention technique.

A visit from Mickey :
The peanut butter solution

If the tale (tail?) at the beginning of this chapter sounds at all familiar and you have quickly flipped to this section, don't despair. It is very difficult to eliminate mice completely, but with a little work, you can keep them under control.

Mice are incredibly frisky little creatures. They can scale brick walls, crawl through holes the size of a dime and eat any type of food, most building materials and pretty well anything they can get their teeny paws on. The good news is that they are generally more afraid of you than you are of them and are quickly frightened by your movements. They are, for example, not very likely to curl up in bed with you.

There are basically two things that you can do. One

is to leave out mouse poison, which usually consists of particles like bird seed that are impregnated with anti-coagulants so that the mice hemorrhage internally and die. Nice huh? The problem is that you have absolutely no idea where they are going to die. I tried this method only once. That was the day I stepped out of bed with my bare feet. You got it, nothing is more disgusting.

Bringing us to the second option. Get yourself two or three of the good, old-fashioned, wooden mouse traps. Hopefully they will stop the mice from beating a path to your door and up your walls. Place the traps wherever you see those miniature 'raisins' around the house. Also, best to put them somewhere out of immediate sight and somewhere that you won't step on them (again, advice from personal experience). You might consider behind the fridge, the TV or the stereo. Get yourself a jar of peanut butter and prepare to load.

Now, I realize that many of you are questioning my use of peanut butter, since every three year old kid knows that mice eat cheese. I can't explain it really, but peanut butter has always worked well for me. If you are a traditionalist, by all means, use cheese.

Pull the wire bale back (against the effort of the spring) and pinch it against the wood using your thumb and forefinger. With the other hand, use a knife to smear a tiny dollop of peanut butter on the little metal flap. Work it right into the hole on the flap so that Mickey has to get his nose right in there. Now flip the straight metal

wire over the bale that you are holding back and under
the lip on the flap with the peanut butter on it. Change
your grip to the sides of the wood base (out of harm's
way) and carefully set the trap down on its destination.
Check your trap lines daily.

Aha! I can tell by that smug look on your face that
you have been out checking your trap lines and you are
gloating with success. Victory is sweet. The squeamish
among you may be wondering how to gracefully remove
this little corpse without having to actually touch it.

You are reading the right book, my friend. Pick the
trap up by the sides once again and hold the whole works
(mouse, trap and remaining peanut butter) over a garbage can. Reaching around the mouse, pull back the bail
wire just as you did when you were loading the trap. Give
the whole thing a vigorous shaking and the mouse should
dislodge nicely.

Is your mouse hanging on? Sometimes the metal bale
will put a nasty kink in their little necks. Give the trap
another good shake or two. I have never seen a mouse
that wouldn't let go eventually. Worst case, have a friend
give him a good prod with a blunt instrument while you
hold back the bale. Be sure to reload the trap and wash
your hands when you are done.

Squeamish and/or rich? Throw the whole works out
and buy another trap.

There is never just one...

You may find that you score a whole herd of mice in the first week. Don't gloat. One of the great truths is that no one has just one mouse. Hopefully, things will taper off and you will be down to just a trickle over the long haul. Also, be sure to keep your kitchen clean and avoid leaving food lying around the house. That includes all of you who keep a bag of Nacho-flavoured Cheese Doritos or those indescribably delectable chocolate chip cookies by your bed.

Back in the kitchen, try storing your food in the cabinets above the sink in tightly sealed boxes or jars with lids. Keep pots, pans and the like in the lower cupboards. Now and then wipe up greasy blobs and sweep up crumbs. Just like Mom said, order and cleanliness pay off.

Over time, you will come to enjoy the thrill of the hunt and the incredible feeling of elation that comes from a successful trapping season. While the temptation may be there to save and cure the little pelts, I would suggest that your Davey Crockett time be more productively spent.

Evil roommates.

It is for good reason that this section lies between the one on mice and the one on cockroaches.

Roommates that have, shall we say, less than the ideal chemistry, can make for a miserable existence. Start right, choose with care. One of the biggest sore points tends to be the level of cleanliness. Few things can be as aggravating as cleaning up after a slob. If you are the one doing endless piles of other people's dishes, taking out the garbage and picking the underwear off the fridge, you can sympathize.

Keep in mind that with three roommates, each will claim to doing most of the cleaning. The mathematical proof of this is a little complex, but trust me. By the time you get to second year algebra, you will understand that it is not possible to have three people, each of whom does all the cleaning.

Try to see the places that your potential roommates live in now. History is still the best predictor of future performance. (Didn't Dad say something like this when it comes to boyfriends – or girlfriends?)

If you have roommate grief, try to have a household meeting to reason with them. Get your feelings out early, before they build up inside and you do a Stephen King number on them. If no amount of reason, discussion, coercion or negotiation will get roommates to straighten up their act, you will have to get rid of them to preserve your sanity.

Try foisting them off on an enemy of the opposite sex, in the hopes that they will move in together. Band together with the good roommates to try and terrorize them out. Leave a half pound of ripe Limburger Cheese under their bed, or a small dead fish in their backpack. Change the locks. Do what it takes. Above all, remember that roommates, like parents, must be carefully chosen to avoid a lifetime of problems.

La Cucaracha?

Did it scurry across the tub? Leap out of your jar of flour? Dart out of the baseboards? Cockroaches are ugly little pests and they can get into almost anything, since they don't have that dime-sized hole restriction that so severely handicaps mice from invading your entire humble home.

Once again, it's time to visit your friendly hardware store to check out the selection of sprays and potions that you can spread around to rid yourself of these beasts. They seem to enjoy damp and dirty climates, so try to keep your bathroom and kitchen clean and dry. If they are really persistent, talk to your landlord or landlady about having the place sprayed by the nice men in the white overalls with the big tanks strapped to their backs.

Legal problems

For whatever reason, things have gone grossly awry. Your roommates have skipped out on you without leaving rent money. At a Super Bowl party, an uninvited soul, overcome with youthful excess, bashed his head through the drywall in the hallway. Someone left the bathtub running and it overflowed into the kitchen.

Whatever happened, happened. The point is, you now have the building manager breathing down your neck and muttering all kinds of things about paying for damages, lawsuits and the like. What to do?

First of all keep your cool. These things always turn out to be much tamer than you originally expected. Lawsuits seldom materialize and time remains the best healer of all ills. Remember too, that lawsuits are an expensive business for both sides. The landlord or the landlady knows that launching a lawsuit is a several thousand dollar proposition and those kinds of costs represent several times the maximum amount that they could get out of you, a broke student.

Shrug off the lawsuit and present a positive helpful image. Try to reason. Is there something that you can do to help set things right? They are unlikely to hold your feet to the fire if there is a sense that you are trying to be helpful. A little genuine remorse helps too.

If things remain sticky, check the government pages of the phone book for the tenant rights groups. A few phone calls should put you in touch with the right department. Usually there is some sort of organization that will help you out. You will also find that in the landlord and tenant laws found in Canada and the United States (they may be one country by the time you read this) heavily favour the tenant. If things make it as far as the court room, you likely have nothing to worry about.

Student hovel, birthplace of student memories

Remember that your new student hovel will be the place that will house not only you, but all of your student memories. Choose it with care, but not too much care. A few small disasters will make for good stories in later years.

**CHAPTER
2**

=

Fiscal
Frenzy

=

Tackling
the cash flow
challenge

As Valley Girls went, your sister did have a certain business flair, depressing as it was to admit. It was two years ago now that you packed up your rusty VW Beetle and headed off to enjoy life in a dormitory, with a pile of overdue assignments, empty cupboards and a roommate with gas. She had packed her gear into the red Alfa Romeo that she won in the art gallery raffle and headed to California where "people aren't dweebs".

In her eyes, college education was definitely for losers. Not a surprising reaction from a woman who punctuated her expressions of distaste with "eeeewwww" and her oh-so-important approval with "right on" (a protracted emphasis on the "right").

Did she ever sweat outside of aerobics class? Did "dirt" only mean gossip to her? Could she consider the possibility that "on sale" did not mean a trip aboard a yacht? Most puzzling of all, how did she get cash to develop such an affinity to her?

The first letters that you received describing her new business were the limit. Just the idea of her running her own business was akin to Madonna writing a GMAT. The first Christmas following her start up, you had sent her a Crispy Crunch chocolate bar, the only gift that was within budget. Textbooks, tuition and rent had decimated your carefully crafted budget. That single Crispy Crunch meant missing out on your supermarket allotted quota of 4 boxes of Kraft Dinner on a 69 cent special. You had hoped that she knew that you could afford more than a chocolate bar, and that you had sent it as a joke.

The (real) Gucci watch that arrived in return was a sobering indication that sis was a success in The Valley.

No schooling, no brains. Just a blonde pony tail and an affinity for all that's cool. But Tofusicles? Who'd have thought that there could be money in her idea of frozen tofu on a stick in the shape of celebrities?. Ever since David Letterman showed up eating one of her tofu treats on his show, the concept had taken off. Cher was spotted on Rodeo drive licking a tofu likeness of herself, while Hanna-Barbera was considering a joint venture with your sister, based on the Flintstones movie where they would sponsor a line of Flintsicles in the shape of Fred, Barney, Wilma, Betty, Dino and the kids. Clearly the whole concept of "Selebrity Sicles" was a winner. Hollywood was hooked. The truth was all too apparent. Sis was the rage of California and you were left in school, lost somewhere between Wuthering Heights and Macroeconomics.

As your stomach growled, a plume of black smoke rose from your tape deck, stopping Bruce Springsteen halfway down Thunder Road. The sudden death of your stereo was punctuated by the dull thud of your mailbox flap. The postman deposited the latest clump of bills, destined to wait helplessly for their overdue-notice-buddies to arrive and accompany them quietly atop the dusty refrigerator.

Financial Trackmeet
for Struggling
Students

For every million dollar idea out there and every Tofusicle entrepreneur, there are thousands of starving students who must carefully scrimp, save and budget to meet such lofty lifestyle enhancements as a bag of chocolate chip cookies and an extra Long Island Iced Tea at the campus pub.

Keeping your finances on track through your school years need not be an onerous task. It does require a little planning, a dash of record keeping and an ability to painfully forgo today's excesses to avoid tomorrow's mountains of student debts, which in turn free up the cash that you will need for formula, diapers and strollers down the road. What could be more reasonable?

The Budget

I know. I have you cringing already. Two thirds of you folks have already flipped ahead to re-read "Examining the Student Body", preferring to let your financial Armageddon assume the dimensions of its choosing. It will. I know, because mine did.

Begin by making a simple planning work sheet like the one shown opposite.

If you have a computer and are a spreadsheet fan (or would like to become one) you can easily set up this type of worksheet as a way of keeping on track. As a side benefit, the exercise will sharpen your skills and, when you graduate and are job-interviewing, will allow you to say, "...spreadsheet skills, are you kidding, of course I have spreadsheet skills."

Dissecting the cash flow planning worksheet

The INCOME section shows all possible sources of income through the school year. It might include an opening balance of savings from a summer job, expected cheques enclosed in a letter from Aunt Mabel, pay cheques from a part time job over the course of the school year, scholarships or student loans or grants from the government (we can all dream, can't we?). Put these headings down the left side and jot the corresponding amounts under

SIMPLE PLANNING WORKSHEET

		SEPT.	OCT.	NOV.	DEC.
	OPENING BALANCE	$ 2,100	$ 650	$ 305	$ -15
INCOME ↑	PAYCHEQUE	75	75	75	75
	MOM	50	50	50	100
	GOV'T LOAN	100	100	100	100
	RICH DATES	75	0	0	0
	TRUST	150	150	150	150
	EMPTIES	15	20	25	30
↓	OTHER?	10	10	10	100 (now mom!)
*	TOTAL	$2575	$1055	$715	$540
EXPENSES ↑	FOOD	$ 175	$ 150	$ 125	$ 125
	BOOZE	$ 175	200	225	200
	RENT	300	300	300	300
	TUITION	1000	—	—	—
	DATES	50	50	50	0
	BOOKS ETC.	200	25	15	10
↓	OTHER	25	25	15	10
*	TOTAL	$ 1925	$ 750	$ 730	$ 645
!!!	BAD NEWS	$ 650	$ 305	$ -15	$ -105 ouch!

the month column when they are most likely to material-ize.

The EXPENSE section shows all possible places where you might spend your cabbage. For the categories shown down the left hand side, use whatever ones that you spend money on. This not only calls for honesty, it requires either a superb memory or a quick pencil to keep track of just where the dollars disappear.

If you are assaulted with wedding invitations, add a section called Wedding Gifts. If you would rather die than give up skiing, rough in something for lift tickets and gas money. Write the whole thing up in pencil because, well, even with all of the best planning, money does have a mind of its own. By setting up a column (the columns are the vertical ones, rows go sideways) for each month of the school year, you will be able to get a handle on when the cash comes in and when it goes out, thus avoiding those embarrassing moments of being caught eating cat food or re-using toilet paper during a period of temporary insolvency.

Got down all of the income and expense items for each month? Now check them all for reasonableness. Fifty bucks a month for food might be a little light. Is that twenty that you have penciled in for monthly entertainment and cocktails really going to hold out? Revised some numbers did we? Great. Now try adding up total incomes and expenses for each month and then for the whole school year.

More income than expense? Beauty. All we'll have to do is make sure that the money is there when you need it. Uh oh. Expenses a little higher than income? We will need more money. There is a section for each of you...

Balancing Cash Flows

If it appears that you have more money available for the school year than you have allocated for your expenses, pinch yourself to make sure that you aren't dreaming. Check to ensure that your math is correct and that you haven't left out any expense categories.

Still with me? OK. Now try to build a running balance for each month to see if the money is there when you will need it. Take your opening balance in your account at the beginning of September and add the total income that you anticipate through the month. Now subtract your September expenses and put the result in the Cash Balance box. For October, carry forward September's Cash Balance to October's opening balance and add October's income, subtract its expenses and put the result under October's Cash Balance. Do the rest of the months.

Oops. Did you get a negative number some place? Those are the spots where you are going to run short. Can you borrow a few bucks from Aunt Mabel to make it through these tight times? Can you pre-pay some bills during the months when you have a little extra cash, or stretch some payments until the following month? Any way of earning a little extra cash to tide you through? Make whatever adjustments you can and recalculate your cash balances.

If you are working on paper, you now have a big pile of that black eraser stuff on your page. You spreadsheet people have laid down a solid foundation of experience to work at one of the big vulture fund outfits in New York.

Need More Money?

You are not alone! Worrying about finances can sap all the fun out of your college days. To remedy the problem, you will have to either do some judicious pruning of your expenditures or devise some crafty scheme to make some extra money.

Expenses are usually the best place to start. Take a good look at food, booze and entertainment to begin with. Endless trips to junk food emporiums can really add up. A home made tuna fish sandwich requires a little extra planning, but a loaf of bread, a couple of tins of tuna and a little mayo will keep you eating all week for the price of a single lunch at the fast food outlet of your choice. Over the course of a month, saving four dollars a day, you could save a hundred bucks or more.

With eight months to the school year and say, a four year program, you could save three grand just by making your own lunch. Sounds crazy, but graduating with three thousand less debt is a nice treat for anyone who has suffered the lengthy pain of paying off school debts. Even if it means eating a lot of tuna fish. What the hell, for three grand you could rotate in a little peanut butter and jam.

Naturally, if you can save that much on lunch, imagine what you could do with just a little restraint on entertainment. Beer and liquor are usually about one quarter the cost to buy at a store than to drink in a bar. By saving two or three bucks a drink over the course of your schooling, you might be able to dramatically ease your cash flow problems and shave another three or four thousand in post-school debts.

Try throwing parties rather than going to campus pubs. Of all the suggestions that I could make to save money, I think that you will agree that throwing parties is likely to be the least painful. Throwing the party at your place, means that you will be the beneficiary of all the empties (additional cash) and food leftovers. As a side benefit, any spilled Tequila that works its way into the floor boards may help to hold down the cockroach population, and keep the termites at bay. (They're all tee-totalers, and get upset when they accidentally get sloshed.)

There are dozens of other ways to save money while at school, following are a couple more suggestions that will help:

•   Consider getting a bicycle and using it for transportation to and from school. Bikes are less than ideal in the rain, for transporting dates or moving into apartments, but with a good knapsack, they can do the trick most of the time. Save about five hundred or more per school year on buses and at least a couple of thousand over driving a car. Side benefit: great way to get in a little extra cardio-vascular exercise and reduce the number of wisecracks about your chicken legs.

•   Roommates Vs solo accommodation. If you can handle a little extra company, you can slash your costs of accommodation almost in half. Check for weird habits, strange hours and significant others that don't seem to have homes of their own before taking the plunge. Through careful roommate selection, you may be able to gain access to high quality leftover food, a substantial second wardrobe, use of a car or even a stereo and TV. I once roomed with a jazz keyboardist and saved dramatically on concert-going.

The other way to ease the pinch is to earn a little extra money while you are at school. There are innumerable ways of doing this and they run the gamut from the conventional to the not so conventional. Here are a few ideas:

• Comb through the awards and scholarship sections of your school calendar. Often there are scholarships that you can apply for that relate to level of need, career interests, city of birth and lord knows what all else. Often, there are a number of these awards that don't require a superior intellect. Bit of a long shot? Maybe. But it beats buying lottery tickets.

• Check out the availability of jobs tutoring courses. Apply to tutor courses that you have done well on in the past. Often these jobs pay well and in some cases involve simply marking papers of the poor sots who are still taking the course. They often pay a fixed amount for the term, but if you really motor as you mark papers and the like, you can work your way up to a superb hourly rate. As a side benefit, it's a great item to add to your resume. It shows your industrious side.

• Consider working at a campus pub and cafeteria. Waiting tables or bartending allows you to earn tips that are likely more than you would make on other part time jobs. It can also be a fun job that will give you a break from the books. Speaking of books, there might even be a bit of part time work at the library. No tips, but you might learn where to find books when you need them.

• How about a small company of your own? Building your own enterprise while at school will help you develop some business skills, earn extra money and impress the hell out of them during interviews for a 'real' job. Some easy-to-start ideas include window cleaning, house painting, odd jobs, preparing tax returns, car washes and whatever else you can make a buck at with minimal materials. If you can get a few people working for you, you may not need a 'real' job.

• The government. Ah yes, you say. But the government is broke and they have no money whatsoever. Shhh! Keep it down. Of course the government is broke. Yes they do have a massive debt. Indeed they top it off with crushing annual deficits. But here's the really neat part: they don't know that yet. That's why they continue to ring up the big deficits.

After all, if they can still shell out for research into the mating habits of fruit flies and use government helicopters to go on golf trips, what difference would a few thou for you make? Exactly. Before you launch into a lifetime of shelling out to our friends in the nation's capital, why not investigate the student grant and loan offerings that might be available to help you make it through school. Contact the office of student affairs at your school for info on what programs are out there and how to apply.

• The summer job. While a summer job isn't going to help you much during the school year, it's a good idea to do a little planning ahead for next year. When examining possibilities of different student jobs, be sure to consider the kind of money that they are paying. The highest paid students easily earn three or four times as much as their starving counterparts, allowing them to buy groceries from the regular shelves rather than the clearance sections.

Back to the Budget

All Right. So we have solved our financial worries. At least we have on paper. How do we make sure that everything goes as planned? There is a simple reason why budgets get derailed. It's easy to spend money. It's one of those relentless, ugly truths about life. Like gravity. Or entropy. Ice cream melts. The kitchen floor gets sticky. It rains on the long weekend. Money disappears.

Technically money can't actually disappear on its own. Unless you live in New York City where anything can disappear. By keeping a very close eye on it, you can ensure that your cash hemorrhages are kept to a minimum.

For a month, try writing down everything that you spend over the course of a day. (OK, OK, try doing it for a week.) You will be amazed at the extra awareness that it brings to the process. You will also find that it is incredible how much you buy that you could have done without and how much less you spend when you are recording all of the gory details. Relate your expenditure records to the budget that we built at the start of this chapter to get an idea of how realistic your monthly expenditure goals are.

Happily, you won't need to record everything that you spend every day for the rest of your life. Doing it for the odd month will prove to be enlightening and will help to keep you on track.

If you find that you are running behind during the course of a month, look for ways to get back on track so that the problem doesn't carry over to the following month. This can make you want to chuck your carefully tuned budget entirely. Worse, it can even make you run up big deficits each year and kid yourself that you will be able to pay for it all one day. That 'one day' has never happened to anyone. By the way, if you live in North America, that last financial strategy will sound more than a little familiar.

Whatever you do, don't be a cheapskate. Look to save money on the things that you can live without. On the other hand, remember that student life just isn't the same without the odd extravagance like something new for the faculty party, a bottle of Single Malt Scotch, a new CD, an impromptu trip to Florida or a new pair of skis.

And on a hot day, what can beat a Tofusicle?

=

Beyond the Care Package

=

Cooking and eating cheap and good

Eight PM. Exhausted, frustrated, smelly and starving.

It has been a helluva day. You handed in your Chemistry lab late and you got back your Math midterm. The professor had marked it in binary rather than in decimal numbers since, she claimed, that was the most efficient way of representing your sub-optimal grade. Your Anthropology assignment due tomorrow, exists only as pristine, white sheets of paper, and it has not yet undertaken the journey to the quiet darkness of the plastic cover that you have so lovingly picked out for it.

The truth is painful, but unavoidable. You haven't started it yet.

The weight of your ill-compiled Visual BASIC program strains the stitching on your knapsack and carves two neat grooves in your shoulders as you continue your trudge home. Darkness begins to fall. The rhythm of your heels on the side walk provides a welcome numbing to the disconsolate events of the day. Your mind searches to find something pleasurable to graze on, some kind of refreshing change from the misery that it has now accepted as reality.

Yesterday's visit from your parents springs to mind. Being with them was an escape back to simpler times. They acted surprisingly normal and didn't make too many comments about your hairstyle, the rips in your jeans, your opposite sex roommates or the apparent cyclone that had mysteriously swept through your apartment. The whole day was a relief from the pressures offered by the daily grind. It was clear they were proud of you for your successes at school so far, although you weren't certain that surprised wasn't the more accurate verb.

Naturally, the best part of the visit was the leftover steak and scalloped potatoes that your mom had brought. It seems that they had organized your birthday dinner last week without you being there. It was a little depressing, but at least they had been kind enough to reward you with the leftovers, including the dessert: Mom's own apple pie.

Suddenly, things are looking up. You adjust the knapsack on your shoulders and your sneakers seem to bound effortlessly toward your apartment. It seems as though a tail wind had developed, helping you on your way. Since it is only a quarter past eight, you would still have time for dinner. Best of all, with mom's leftovers safely in the fridge, there would actually be something to eat. After dinner there would still be time to work on your Anthropology assignment, you kid yourself, knowing that Seinfeld will be on at 9:30. A growl from your stomach reminds you that lunch was a long time ago and there is still fifteen minutes of walking ahead.

Wait. What is that up ahead just above the sidewalk? Steam is rising gently from a huge steak, smothered in mushroom sauce. Nestled next to it is a veritable mountain range of scalloped potatoes. The smells waft temptingly toward you as your eyes strain at the vision ahead. Yes. It is a plate of warm apple pie with a ball of ice cream crouched down, slowly surfing on the crust.

With a shake of your head, the image is gone. Picking up the pace, you jog the last few blocks home.

You hear the sound of the television from your apartment as you bound up the steps. The scene in the kitchen enrages you. The tiny bits of charred black steak on your roommates' face provide the overview. The scalloped potato stains on his shirt fill in the details. His cheeks, stuffed to the limit with apple pie and ice cream, form the conclusive evidence.

Cooking Easy
and Eating Cheap
and Good:
The Solution

Roommates can never be trusted fully, and high-grade leftovers can stress even the closest of friendships, as year end budgets run dry and all roommates stake a claim on that last box of Kraft Dinner that silently stands guard over the barren, paint chipped surfaces of your cupboards.

Food can take a low priority when assignments and exams compete for your attention and even washroom breaks need to be booked two weeks in advance.

To keep 'borrowing' roommates at bay, try booby trapping one or two fridge items to teach 'em a lesson. Punch a hole in the bottom of a beer can and fill it up with pickle juice, covering the hole with some duct tape. Inject that last piece of chocolate cake with dish soap. Be sure to keep a mental map of what is still safe.

Balancing that delicate line between the truly cheap and tasteless and the pricey yet palatable can prove to be a tenuous task. More than cheap and tasty, every student needs a kitchen repertoire that is also easy, quick and good. Read 'nutritious' for good. Pop and chips, burgers and fries are basic stuff but they don't make up the everyday fare that will really keep you going. It's those complex carbohydrates liberally laced with solid greens and other veggies and snacks of fruit, milk and yogurt that are really the bottom line. A bit more spent there in time and money balances out to less time in sick bay and fewer medical prescriptions. But how?

Once again, luckily, you have come to the right book to find all the answers.

Begin at the Survival Rations and work your way up

This chapter is divided into three sections to suit both your tastes and your pocket book. If you find yourself constantly in a hurry, and the queens, kings or presidents on the bills squint when you open your wallet, you will want to prepare most of your chow from the Survival Rations section. Your basic complex carbohydrates: pastas, breads, grains, and vegetables like spuds and carrots do the trick. This type of stuff requires minimal ingredients and can be prepared and wolfed down in less than ten minutes in most cases.

These delightful survival dishes will likely keep you going all term provided you stock up on some vitamin and mineral pills, avoid excessive exertion and get plenty of rest. If signs of scurvy or rickets appear, or if anything swells up or becomes discoloured, see your doctor, shell out the extra cash for ingredients and move up to the next level and prepare to enjoy the Palate Pleasers.

The Palate Pleasers are a collection of college favourites that require a little planning, a working stove and a touch of your personal artistry. They will also require a few ingredients that can bump the cost per serving up beyond one dollar. Some of these creations even taste good. The food will keep you happy and healthy and even mom would approve of the nutrient value.

For those occasions where you need to prepare the very best, flip ahead to the Haute de Cuisine section. There you will find the simmering sauces, the ominous omelets and the flaming fantasies that you will need to ensure the awed dedication from that dream boat that you will unquestionably meet through the methods that I will outline in Chapter Five. But first, work your way through this Chapter.

For generations, people have been on the quest for the food that is the perfect aphrodisiac. Key point to remember: If the student you are chasing is as broke and as starving as you, *any* food will be an aphrodisiac. If nothing else, it will encourage them to keep coming over, if only to eat.

Simple as that. Check your budget, know your tastes, loosen up and experiment a bit, and turn to the section that suits your habits the best. Practice. And, oh yes, Bon Appetit!

The Basics

Before we don our aprons and start spraying flour around the kitchen, let's lay out some basic ground rules and concepts to make the work as simple as possible. These tips will apply to all three levels of cuisine.

Measurement

Cooking can often involve the combination of two or more reagents (often called ingredients by chefs) to create a new substance that you will learn to eat. Of course you will eat it. You made it didn't you? With luck, it will be an enjoyable experience both to cook and to eat. More often than not, it is useful to use the appropriate amount of these reagents to create your dish.

Most cookbooks will tell you what to put in, but they will use ridiculous units of measure like tbsp's, tsp's, cups and the like. The whole thing is a scam that was set up years ago by a secret society of cooks that wanted to set up a cartel on the market.

Throughout this chapter, we will use only three units of measure.

One is the coffee mug, which I will refer to as 'a mug'.

Second unit is 'the spoon'. What kind of spoon? It doesn't matter. Just a spoon.

The third type of measure is 'some'. As in "Add some salt". Or, "Add some vinegar". A couple of good shakes of whatever is dispensing the ingredient ought to do it. Most people cook far too precisely anyway. Quick review - a mug, a spoon and some. Great!

Tools

There are a few items that you will need to create your new gourmet masterpieces, particularly those that will require some cooking. I will keep the list to a minimum, but if you can load up with all of the items below, you will be able to make everything in this chapter.

For most of these items, scour the basement, the kitchen drawers, and in unsuspecting cupboard corners. If you strike out in the basement, check the attic. No luck? Some relatives or kind neighbours probably have duplicates gathering dust. Or you can probably buy everything that you will need at a garage sale, flea market or at one of those discount stores.

1.   A BIG POT. Get one ten or more inches in diameter and five or more inches high. A matching lid will be especially handy. Stainless steel (shiny silver look) is the best since it cleans easily, distributes heat well. Aluminum

ones (not as shiny) will do the job, but they can be tougher to clean. Make sure that your roommates don't rinse out their swim suits in this baby.

2.   A REGULAR POT. About eight inches across (that would be 25.13274122872 in circumference for you math types) and four inches deep with a handle out one side and a matching lid. Again, stainless steel is the best, aluminum will do.

3.   A PYREX PAN. These are square or rectangular clear glass pans that say Pyrex on the bottom. The nine by thirteen inch size is the best, but you can probably live with a nine by nine inch one.

4.   A FRYING PAN. Get one ten to twelve inches in diameter, ideally one of the Teflon coated or Silverstone ones. They are easy to clean. Just don't scratch the surface by using metal implements with it.

5.   A FLIPPER (a.k.a. a spatula). Plastic ones are the best since you won't scratch your nice Teflon pans.

6.   A WOODEN SPOON. Yup, just like the one that grandma used to use on your backside. Check the basement again or pick one up cheap at the corner store.

7.   A COLANDER : Don't start off wrong by calling it a strainer. Get a plastic one at a grocery or kitchen store. These babies are indispensable for draining noodles, washing fruit and veggies and things. If you progress to the Haute de Cuisine section, you will learn to call it "colander" but for now, we can run with "strainer." In a pinch, you can use an old tennis or squash racket.

8.   PLASTIC LEFTOVER CONTAINERS. These aren't essential, but they are handy for saving your leftovers and keeping the green suede off them. Tupperware works well, as do any of the sets available at the grocery store. Or save old yogurt containers.

9. TIN FOIL. Get a big roll to keep you going all term. Very useful when roasting things in your new Pyrex pan.

10. A TOASTER. What better way to make toast? If you can't get one for free, try rummaging around at some garage sales until you find one that you like. Be sure to plug it in to make sure that it heats up, before you buy.

11. A SHARP KNIFE. One with a smooth sharp blade about eight inches long will do the trick.

12. A SERVING CLOTH. A white towel from the Recreation Centre will do nicely. Once a month return it back to the recreation centre and pick up a clean one. That way you aren't stealing anything. Just make sure that when you finally graduate, you take the last towel back. You should probably also set up a scholarship or something at your school so that some lucky kid that follows you can actually go out and buy a proper serving cloth, you cheapskate!

13. A WHISK: This is really in the graduate department of the Haute de Cuisine, but we'll show it to you here, to start you off easy with just a look. Later we'll demonstrate.

Cleanup tips : Take the tips, there's no escape

Following are a few ideas to help you forge your way through the mountains of grimy dishes that can result from all of this cooking:

1. While waiting for something to finish cooking, take a moment to clean up your work area, wash any utensils and at least get the major items soaking in some hot water and dish soap. If it takes a long time to cook, shake

out some of the drawer crumbs too. You find interesting stuff that way.

2.   Never leave an item to dry out, harden and endure a metamorphosis to something unworldly, especially things like sauces and noodle pots. They can become virtually impossible to clean. Get everything soaking as soon as possible after completion of the meal.

3.   For really tough pots, scrape the major hunks out with a spoon and let the pot soak for at least one hour with hot water and dish soap. Then try to clean it with one of those plastic bristle scrubbers. If that doesn't do it, try putting a little dish soap and a couple mugs of water in it and let it cook on a low element for an hour.

Or try a few spoonfuls of baking soda and a couple of mugs of water. Bring to a boil and watch the brown scrunge bubble up. Don't forget about it! Then try the scrubber again. Should do it. Be very careful with these ideas, by the way. Too much heat, water, baking soda, or dish soap and the whole thing will foam up and cover your whole kitchen with whatever was in the pot.

4.   Keep things moist while you are cooking them. If something starts to look dry or smell burnt, add some water to unstick it from the pan and re-moisten the food.

That's it. You are ready to begin.

Survival Rations

You only foray into a kitchen to grab a beer? You think that The Cloves of Garlic are some sort of a religious order? Compote was the guy who wrote the murder mysteries? OK. No need for panic, you have come to the right place.

This is the section designed for the gastronomically inept and the constantly broke and hungry.

The Fried Egg Sandwich

I can almost taste it now. I know that it doesn't sound like much, but give it a try. They are tasty and the total ingredient cost for this breakfast/lunch/dinner/snack is about thirty cents.

Ingredients

One egg

Some mayonnaise

*(if you are asking how much is 'some' you need to
re-read the beginning of this chapter).*

Two slices of brown grainy bread

(the white stuff is for wimps).

Some pepper and salt.

Some butter.

Tools

Fry pan.

Flipper.

Stove that works or at least a hot plate.

Directions

Timing is everything. Turn on your stove to medium high (or about six on a scale from one to nine). Place your frying pan on the heated element and add some butter about the size of a quarter. Wait for it to start swimming around.

As soon as it moves, drop your bread in the toaster and turn it on. Run back to the stove and you should see the butter starting to bubble. As soon as it does, crack the egg into the pan and use the corner of your flipper to break the yolk so that the yellow part runs into the white part. Shake some salt and pepper on the gooey part.

Give it a minute or so and then slide your flipper under the egg and flip it. Turn off the heat, run over to the toaster, remove the bread and slather some mayonnaise on one piece. Scoop up your egg with your flipper and lay it on the bread and then quickly cover it with the other piece of bread. Wolf it down quickly while it is still hot.

Awesome.

Kraft Dinner Plus

What chapter on student cuisine could be complete without directions for making Kraft Dinner? I will even include some tips for improving it that even the people from Kraft won't tell you.

Ingredients

One box of Kraft Dinner

Some hot dogs or a tin of beans

(optional, but a big improvement over plain KD)

Some butter

Some powdered onion soup mix

(optional, but again a real enhancement)

Some milk.

Tools

A regular pot

A plastic strainer

A wooden spoon

Directions

Turn one of your stove elements to high (or nine or ten or Max).

Pour four mugs of water into your regular pot and place it on the heated element. Take some hot dogs and slice them into pieces about one inch long and set them off to one side. Or open a small tin of beans. For a little variety, you can slice the dogs on a 45 degree angle rather than straight across to make them look like the vegetables in Chinese Food. Add some salt to the water in the pot.

When the water boils (big bubbles in the water and lots of steam rising), open the box of Kraft Dinner and remove the cheese sauce mix. Dump noodles and sliced hot dogs (beans are added later with the Kraft cheese stuff) into the boiling water and let the whole works boil for about twelve minutes or until the noodles are tender.

If you are not sure when they are done, just pull one out with your wooden spoon, blow on it to cool, and then taste it. Optionally, you can toss a noodle against a wall. If it sticks it's done. If it falls off the wall, try giving it another couple of minutes. By using the toss method on a regular basis, you will have a post modern pasta sculpture on the wall by the time you graduate.

When the noodles are ready, turn the element to low, remove the pot from the heat and dump noodles and dogs into the strainer which should be sitting in the sink. Run some hot water over the noodles and dogs while they are in the strainer to wash off all of the — well, whatever it is that needs to be washed off.

Now, add some butter to the bottom of the empty, but still hot pot and place it back on the element that you have turned down to low heat. Dump the rinsed and drained noodles and dogs back into the pot. Open the cheese sauce mix package and dump it in too. You can add beans at this point. Then add one eighth of a mug of milk and stir the whole works up until there are no big bright orange globs of cheese sauce mix.

Now here's the trick. Toss in about one eighth of a mug of powdered Onion Soup mix and stir it in as well. Serves two. Lovely.

Leftovers? No problem. Dump the extras into your handy plastic containers and stick the whole works right into the fridge. In a rush in the morning, start your day with an energy blast: hot KD on toast. You prefer hot oatmeal? Fine. Toss the leftover KD with salad greenery and serve yourself a Cold KD Salad. Now that's cool.

Ensalada Estudiente

How about a little side salad to go with your main dish? Also, not a bad idea to at least have a few vegetables hanging around, just in case your parents come to visit. Impresses Aunts and Uncles too. Whatever your motives, you are looking for an easy-to-make salad with dressing. You have truly arrived when you can master the Salade Estudiente. Don't be alarmed by the long list of goodies, just look after one at a time.

Ingredients

Some lettuce

A green pepper

A tomato

Some celery

Some of whatever other vegetables you can find.

Some ketchup

Some olive oil

(the oil and vinegar are expensive, but they will probably last you all year)

Some salt

Some sugar

Some wine vinegar

(plain white vinegar is for washing windows)

Tools

A plastic strainer

A sharp knife

A coffee mug

Directions

Give all of your vegetables a good washing with cold water to remove all of the crud that may have become lodged on them during transit. Rip off small pieces of the lettuce and toss it into your plastic strainer in the sink.

Slice the green pepper in half and pull out all of the seedy parts in the middle and pitch them in the garbage. Rinse out the insides and then slice the pepper into lengthwise strips and then cross wise to make little squares about one half inch. Put the pepper squares into the plastic strainer with the lettuce.

Pull the green thing out of the end of your tomato and slice it in half from where you pulled out the green thing to the other 'pole' of the tomato. Place the two halves face down and slice 'em in half again. Repeat one more time. Now turn these wedges sideways and cut them each into four pieces. Throw the works into your plastic strainer.

Slice the last 1/4 inch off each end of your celery and throw them out, then trim off the leaves. Slice the remaining stalk into thin slices crosswise and toss them in the strainer. As a rule of thumb, the harder the vegetable (carrots or celery) the smaller the slices so that you don't ruin your dental work or that of your dinner guests.

For the dressing, you can save money by making your own. In a coffee mug, pour one quarter mug of ketchup, one quarter mug of water, one spoon of sugar, one spoon of wine vinegar, one spoon of olive oil and some salt and pepper. Stir the whole works up and presto, you have dressing.

Toss the vegetables around in the strainer with your hands, put some in a bowl and splash some of your dressing on top. Excellent. For variety, try throwing some grated cheese and sliced ham on top. Don't forget to keep the leftovers in your plastic food savers in the fridge.

Le Fishstick

Ahh, the salt spray, the Rhyme of the Ancient Mariner or perhaps an old Gilligan's Island episode have got you in the mood for some fruits of the sea. Never mind the idea that you can't afford seafood. Le Fishstick is an easy, economical way to enjoy the catch of the day.

Ingredients
One box of frozen fish sticks

Tools

Some tin foil

An oven

Directions

Heat the oven up to 350 F. From your box of frozen fish sticks, remove as many as you think you can eat. Set them on a sheet of tin foil, shiny side up. Wrap the foil over top of the fish sticks to make a neat little package with the shiny side of the foil facing inward to the fish sticks. Put the whole works on the rack in the oven for twenty minutes. Remove and taste a little piece. If they are still cold, send them back in for another fifteen minutes. If they are warm, but not hot, try ten minutes. If in doubt, read the directions on the box.

When they are fully heated, serve them up on a plate. You might want to make a little seafood sauce by combining one eighth of a mug of relish with one eighth of a mug of mayonnaise. Try serving with Salade Estudiente as a side dish.

Palate Pleasers

Got a little more time on your hands. A little extra cash. Eaten all the recipes in the Survival Rations section twelve times? Lost more than ten pounds? Sounds like you're ready for the Palate Pleasers, a selection of recipes as delightful to make as they are to eat. Here we go.

Spuds Niçoise

Potatoes are incredibly cheap, nourishing and filling. In short, its a good idea to keep a big bag of 'em handy. And carrots are incredibly cheap, nourishing (all that beta carotene you been hearing about) and satisfy the need to crunch. But back to the spuds. The possibilities are endless, so I will give you the basics and a few variations to get you started...

Ingredients
Some spuds (I prefer the red skins)
Some butter
Some cheese OR
Some barbecue sauce OR
Ketchup and soy sauce mix (60:40) OR
Some sour cream or yogurt

Tools

Big pot

Plastic strainer

Frying pan

Directions

Fill the big pot one third full of water and set it on a burner at high heat. Add a sprinkle of salt to the water. While waiting for the water to boil, wash the spuds under cool water and use a plastic dish scrubber to clean off all the dirt. If they are really filthy, you may have to change the water and give them a second scrubbing. Cut the potatoes once lengthwise and once widthwise, leaving them, you guessed it, in quarters.

When the water is boiling, add potato quarters until the water comes within about 2" of the top edge of the pot. Leave the spuds to boil for about 20 minutes or until a fork slides in fairly easily. Don't let them get mooshy.

When they are cooked, turn the burner down to medium high and dump the spuds out into your plastic strainer in the sink and let them dry out a bit. Toss a spoonful of butter into your frying pan and set it on that medium high burner.

Slice the quartered potatoes into thinner wedges, letting them fall into the frying pan. Turn them every couple of minutes or so, adding extra butter to the pan if they start to burn. Sprinkle on some salt and pepper. When they are all nice and golden brown you have a number of options:

Option 1.

Lay some slices of cheese on them and let
the cheese melt. Serve.

Option 2.

Douse them in barbecue sauce. Serve.

Option 3.

Douse them in sour cream or plain yogurt. Serve.

Option 4.

You could have cooked some rounds of carrots too
and done options 1, 2, 3.

Option 5.

Spoon on cottage cheese and douse with
chopped tomatoes and onions.

Option 6.

Toss the cooked spuds with slivers of salami,
or bacon, or any leftover meats.

The possibilities are endless. Almost anything that you can find in your fridge can be drizzled, sprinkled, or doused on top. Create your own spud sensations. Got a microwave or a workable oven, how about baked spuds? Give them the old fork test, split them open and squeeze gently to puff out the fluffy insides and pile on anything that's around. Literally a meal in one. Another delicious student original.

Rice Variations International

White rice or brown rice, eaten with chopsticks, fork or spoon, it really satisfies, goes on top of, underneath or mixed with almost anything, keeps for a week, cooks up to three times its volume. How's that for healthy, cheap, and versatile as survivor food? Now for the quick and easy part.

Difficult as it is for me to part with long-treasured secrets, here it is. The cheap, quick method for perfect rice every time. You will need a pot. Remember that rice triples its volume in cooking. Simple then: one mug of rice and three mugs of cold water. Cover the pot and turn up the heat to "high."

Watch it. As soon as the first hiss of steam appears, turn to the lowest possible heat, even to putting a metal trivet under the pot. Now go do other things and let it cook and mind it's own business for 20 minutes.

Turn off the heat. Lift the cover. AAAAAHHHH every grain of rice plump and separate. No mooshies here, and no leftover water either. Some ideas:

• Throw in a tin of any beans (drained and rinsed) and sprinkle some cheese on top: Vegetarian Dinner

• Toss the cooked rice with some heated veggies. Nice with a sliced hard egg on top.

• Toss the cooked rice with prepared instant pudding made with milk. Borrow a half mug of raisins and toss them in too: Rice Pudding.

• Toss the cooked rice with some soy sauce, some chopped bacon (or whatever), some onions and some celery: Fried Rice.

Toss the cooked rice with a leftover crumbled up hamburger and some ketchup or tomato sauce: Burger Stew.

Now that you got the basic and some variables, try your own. Go ahead, impress yourself.

KD Casserole for Two

Aha! You recognize the initials KD as standing for Kraft Dinner and you are indeed very observant. This little charmer is likely to really blow your guests away. Not much tougher to make than regular KD either.

Ingredients

2 mugs of frozen mixed vegetables
(the California ones with the cauliflower, crinkle cut carrots and broccoli are the best, but any kind, including the good old peas, carrots and corn, will do)
1 box of Kraft Dinner
Some crackers, potato chips or corn chips or whatever
Some cheese
(whatever you got - Parmesan, Cheddar, Swiss, whatever)
Some butter

Tools

Big pot
Pyrex pan
Plastic strainer
Oven

Directions

Fill your big pot about 1/2 full of water. Add a dash of salt and turn the oven burner to its maximum heat. If you have some cooking oil around you can toss in a spoon of it to help stop the noodles from sticking. While waiting for the water to boil, open the box of Kraft Dinner and remove the envelope with the cheese sauce mix. Set it aside. Measure out 2 mugs of frozen mixed vegetables and set them aside (either in two coffee mugs or in a bowl.)

When the water reaches a boil, dump in the box of Kraft Dinner noodles, and note the time. Give it a stir every now and again to keep the little suckers from sticking to the bottom of the pot (they will anyway). After six minutes, dump in the two mugs of frozen vegetables, and give everything another six minutes to boil and swap flavours. Turn off the burner you were using and set the oven to 350 F.

Dump the cooked vegetables and the noodles into your plastic colander and give them a good rinse with hot water. Add a spoonful of butter to your big pot and dump the noodles and the vegetables back in along with the contents of the cheese sauce mix packet. Add 1/4 mug of milk and mix it in as well. Yum. Give it a good stir.

Take out your Pyrex pan and dump the contents of your big pot into it, spreading it all around so that it is an even depth throughout. Crumble your crackers and/or chips in your hand and sprinkle them on top of the noodles and vegetables in the pan. If the cheese you are using is already in small particles (like powdered Parmigiana) sprinkle it evenly on top of the crackers, otherwise, slice the cheese into fine strips and lay the strips evenly on top of the crackers. Put the pan in the oven and leave it for fifteen minutes, or until the cheese is melted on top.

Turn the oven off and use your serving cloth to remove your casserole from the oven. Gently slide it onto plates using your flipper, making sure that you get enough cracker and cheese topping for both you and your guest. Enjoy!

Some International KD Variations

What's more versatile than KD? Here are some surprising versions contributed by readers. And good too. They mainly call for mixing, boiling skills and add a few tricks worth noting.

• A party from leftovers of Chinese food takeout? Sure. Do the usual KD number but at the end toss in the leftover Fried Rice, bits of Broccoli and Beef and even the Sweet and Sour Spareribs overlooked in the carton. Stir up with a fork. Get it nice and hot then serve. You can pass the leftover Soy Sauce and extra Sweet and Sour Sauce. Just watch out for those rib bones.

• Brown up a mug of thinly sliced onions with some oil and a sprinkle of sugar. Hey now there's a chef's secret if I ever saw one.(Makes the onions golden brown) Throw in some nicely sliced fresh mushrooms and toss around till they smell irresistible. Meanwhile have the KD noodles cooking up a storm. Drain. Toss with the onions and mushrooms and sprinkle the cheese stuff on top.

• This version calls for some packaged curry paste from the Oriental Grocery Store. Heat some curry paste with some oil. Add that to the precooked noodles from KD and even some heated frozen veggies. Toss together. Serve with the KD cheese stuff and some chopped peanuts on top.

Bluefish Fettucini

OK, I lied. Le Fishstick are starting to taste like nothing more than frozen fish sticks and you are hungering for some REAL seafood. Naturally, your budget is no better and your cooking skills are still less than world class. Bluefish Fettucini will fool them every time. It is a similar concept to KD Casserole and just as easy. The beauty of it is that it uses skills that you have already developed (boiling and stirring) and yet it will let you dramatically expand your repertoire. Let's begin...

Ingredients

1 package of frozen bluefish fillets
(I use Highliner brand)
be sure to defrost them in the fridge overnight
4 mugs of noodles
*(any kind will do, check the Italian section of your
grocery store and buy a big bag).*
1 mug of milk

Some butter
Some salt
1 small can of mushroom soup

Tools

Big pot
Medium pot
Plastic strainer

Directions

Turn one of your stove burners on to its maximum setting. Oh yeah. You are probably wondering how much this recipe will make. I don't know. I could swear I use the same amount of ingredients every time and sometimes there is enough for just me and sometimes I fill up a couple of those plastic storage containers. If you are feeding two or three, you should be OK. If you are feeding four, maybe toss in an extra mug of noodles.

Fill your big pot approximately 1/2 full of water and set it on the element to boil. While you are waiting for the water to boil, measure out 4 mugs of noodles and set them aside.

Turn a second burner to its low setting and add one mug of milk, the can of mushroom soup and the bluefish fillets. Stir gently so that the fish, the milk and the mushroom soup meld together into an ambrosial delight. Add salt and pepper to taste.

If this sauce starts to bubble heavily, turn it down a

notch or two. Don't forget to give it a stir every now and again, or it will become a charred meltdown.

The water in the big pot is probably boiling furiously by now. Great. Dump in your four mugs of noodles, boiling them for about 20 minutes or until they taste about right (not too hard, not too mooshy).

When the noodles are done, turn off the burner you were using and turn the sauce burner up to about mid way. Dump your noodles into your plastic strainer (colander, just a reminder to keep you on your toes) and give them a good rinse with hot water. Shake them vigorously to remove all the excess water. Load the noodles onto plates and add a good sized dollop of your bluefish sauce on top. Serve with a cold glass of beer. Superb.

Gotta Lasagna

Perfezione! Time for a little Italiano cuisine. Here is a lasagna that isn't terribly quick to make, but it is nutritious, tasty and it will keep you fed for at least a week. Or if you are entertaining dinner guests, this will do for about six of 'em. If you are considering this for a special date with your newest heartthrob, trust me. Nothing is a surer route to someone's heart than a good homemade lasagna.

Ingredients
1 bag of lasagna noodles.
1 small can of mushroom soup

*(good to toss in to almost anything, so stock up
when they put it on sale)*
1 big jar of spaghetti sauce
*(ideally, get one with mushrooms and all the trim-
mings)*
1 good sized package of Mozzarella cheese
*(take your calculator and work out the unit cost
on this stuff - it's always a rip off)*
1 spoon of butter

Tools
Big pot
Medium pot
Plastic strainer
Wooden spoon

Directions
Fill your big pot 1/2 full of water, on a stove burner set to high. Drop one spoonful of butter into the water. This will help to keep the noodles from sticking together. While waiting for it to boil, dump your mushroom soup and spaghetti sauce into your medium pot and add about 1/2 mug of water. Set it on another burner at medium-low heat. Keep stirring – enter the wire whisk – it until the mushroom soup, water and the spaghetti sauce all blend together nicely.

As soon as the water starts boiling in the big pot, put the lasagna noodles in. Don't tell me, let me guess. Your noodles won't fit in the pot. I've been there, don't panic. Put them in with one end sticking out and give them about a minute to soften up. Push on the exposed end and you should find that they will coil around inside the pot until they are all submerged. Be careful not to burn your fingers while you are noodle wrestling. Give the noodles a stir with your wooden spoon.

Now while everything is boiling and simmering nicely, turn your oven on to 350 F. Take out your Pyrex pan and smear butter all over the inside of it with your fingers. Wash your hands well. In hindsight, you may also want to wash your hands well prior to using them to smear the butter all over the pan. Slice your Mozzarella cheese into thin slices and set aside. Don't forget to keep stirring your sauce to make sure it isn't sticking to the bottom. But it will.

When the noodles have been boiling for about 15 minutes, start tasting them to check for consistency. Toss one against the wall to work on your sculpture. You want them cooked all the way through and just a bit chewy in the centre. When they are done, dump them into your plastic strainer in the sink and rinse them well with warm water.

Now comes the fun part. Lay one layer of noodles in the bottom of your Pyrex pan. If they don't fit, rip off the excess. You can use it somewhere else later. Scoop a nice layer of sauce on top of the noodles. Now, run the next layer of noodles the other direction to help give your lasagna some structural integrity (like plywood). Continue alternating layers of sauce and noodles until:

1. You run out of sauce.
2. You run out of noodles.
3. You get bored.
4. You are dying to find out how the sliced cheese works into all of this.
5. The pan is almost full.

Here comes the cheese. Over your last layer, add a layer of sliced Mozzarella cheese. All right, you say, should I be adding the cheese on top of a layer of noodles or on top of a layer of sauce. There are actually two schools of thought on this, but I would recommend adding the cheese onto the sauce layer. Don't sweat it if you ran out of sauce and had to run the cheese on top of the noodles.

With all of your layers done, open the oven and slide your lasagna onto a rack on about the middle level. Leave it in there for about 15 minutes or until smoke billows out of the oven. Remove using at least one serving cloth. (By the way, important safety tip here. Never use a wet towel to remove something from the oven, they get very hot very fast.) Cut into squares with a knife and use your flipper to serve it onto plates. If you let it all sit for a few minutes while you entertain with some enchanting topic the lasagna will be easier to cut up. It just sticks together better. Serve with either a cold beer or a big glass of milk.

Haute de Cuisine

Ha! You laugh. Those recipes are hardly food. There must be life beyond noodles.

Perhaps your budget is somewhat more liberal with your paltry student loan being sautéed with some extra cash that your Uncle Reginald sent you. Perhaps your tastes yearn for dishes that can only be described adequately in foreign languages.

Maybe you have flunked a couple of years of school

and now, entering your sixth year, you thought that since you are likely to be here for a while, you may as well at least enjoy the food.

You are now ready for an upgrade in tools. For beating eggs, stirring liquid stuff and making the smoothest sauces there's only one tool: the wire whisk. Out with the strainer, bring on the colander. On then, to the Haute de Cuisine!

Ominous Omelet

Having carefully selected your courses so that you never need to be on campus before 11:30 in the morning, you have the time to lounge and enjoy a decent breakfast. How about a superb omelet to savour as you peruse your morning paper?

Ingredients

2 eggs

Some spaghetti sauce

Some whole fresh mushrooms, green peppers
and onions and avocado

Some cheese

(whatever kind you may have handy)

1 spoonful of butter

Tools

Fry pan

Medium pot

Flipper

Bowl

Whisk

Directions

In your medium pot, pour about 1/2 a mug of spaghetti sauce and set to warm on a medium-low burner. Slice up about 3 mushrooms, some slivers of green pepper, cut avocado and onion into thin slices and drop them into the sauce. Give the whole works a very gentle stir. Just heat, don't cook.

Put a small spoonful of butter into your frying pan and set it on a medium-high burner. Crack two eggs into a bowl and whisk them feverishly in a circular motion that brings in air to make them light. When the butter melts and starts to bubble, pour in your freshly whisked eggs. Give the omelet about 2 minutes to cook and then use your flipper to gently work the edges of the omelet free. After about 3 minutes, slide your flipper under the whole omelet and carefully flip it over. I make it sound easy, but that's only because I've been working on it for a while.

If you want to serve this French style, then don't flip the omelet, poke a few holes to let the wet top run under to cook. In France, they like their omelets soft. Me, I like em' cooked.

Pour your sauce over one half of the omelet and use your flipper to roll the sauce-loaded part over itself. Continue rolling it until the whole omelet is like a tube with the sauce inside. OK maybe oozing a bit. Roll it right out of the pan and on to your plate. Lay paper thin slices of cheese over the hot omelet. We call this a 'cheese glaze.' Serve with a sprig of parsley and a Perrier. Toasted bagel is good too.

Spinach Salad Strawberry Surprise

If you were initially keen on Ensalada Estudiente in your first year, but the attraction has worn a little thin, it may be time to move up to another form of greenery. The unique thing about this salad is that you will love it even if you hate spinach. Trust me. As a side benefit, if you tell your parents that you are eating spinach they may decide to send you more money, or at least more kitchen tools.

Ingredients
A big bag of washed spinach *(saves time)*
Some hard cheese *(Cheddar, Gouda, whatever)*
A little box of strawberries
Some orange juice
Some honey
Some salt & pepper

Some nuts *(even some leftover peanuts will work)*

Tools

A plastic colander
A sharp knife
A coffee mug

Directions

No pre-washed spinach? Wash up your spinach in the sink and then let it drip-dry in your colander. (Tennis racket? This is Haut de Cuisine. Did you forget?) Slice your strawberries into quarters and toss them into your big bowl with your now drip-dried spinach. Cut your cheese into little cubes and toss them into your bowl as well.

In a coffee mug pour in about 1/4 of a mug of orange juice, a couple spoons of honey, a spoon of vegetable oil and some salt and pepper.

Use your big knife and your cutting board to chop up your nuts into little pieces (Lorena don't get any new ideas here) and then dump them into the bowl with all the other stuff.

Stir up your dressing and pour some on top of the salad. Give the whole works a good tossing (use a couple of squash racquets if you have no salad tossers) and you are all set. As you assemble this salad, you will want to use your judgment as to how much of each main ingredient you want.

My initial thought would have been to just have a

bowl of strawberries with some honey and orange juice drizzled on top, but trust me, the spinach will grow on you.

Pawsta Purfection

OK, so the spelling is a little weird, but you will notice when dining out at the finer restaurants that there are three different price-related names for this stuff. At an all-you-can eat, side of the road truck stop, they are your basic noodles. As you move closer to a town or built-up area, they are elevated to being called pasta (rhymes with fasta - as in 'can't you drive any...') and the dinner is sold, for say, 6 bucks. When you scan the menu in a really jazzy place and the price soars to $15.95, you will notice that they start calling it Pawsta. I don't know why that is, but a similar thing happens to Sherbet as it becomes more expensive and gets sold as Sorbet.

At any rate, it is time for you to learn how to make your own Pawsta Sauce, and at the same time add to the spice rack.

Ingredients

Some sliced up cheese *(Cheddar, Gouda, or whatever)*
Some butter for the sauce, oil for the Pawsta
Some cornstarch or flour
Some milk *(homo is ideal)*
Some oregano
Some salt and pepper

Some garlic powder
Some noodles with tricky shapes or maybe flavoured
too. *(that will be transformed to Pawsta)*

Tools

Big pot
Medium pot
Big knife
Whisk

Directions

Fill your big pot 1/2 full with water and set it to boil. Add
a spoon of oil and some salt. While you are waiting for the
pot to boil, put 2 spoons of butter in one side of your medium pot and 2 spoons of flour or cornstarch on the other
side. Turn the heat on to medium. When the butter starts
to flow into the flour, get out your whisk and go to it. Before everything starts turning brown, dribble in 4 mugs
of milk and continue to whisk as it thickens. See, no
lumps.

By the way, as soon as your water starts boiling in
the other pot, you can dump in your noodles. The more
advanced the cuisine, the more pots you gotta watch.

Turn up the heat on your sauce to medium-high and
bring it to a boil (big bubbles) and keep whisking the
daylights out of it. Let it boil like that for about 30 seconds or so and then turn it down to medium-low.

Now here's the nifty part: This sauce is called a White

Sauce and you can make anything out of it. If you were to throw in some chocolate, you could create a terrific chocolate sauce. Stir in some concentrated chicken broth (or those neat little cubes that store forever) and you have a lovely creamy chicken sauce. Add some chicken cut up with some veggies and you have Chicken Pot Pie (crustless version). To make a cheese sauce, stir in 1/2 mug of sliced up cheese, some oregano, some salt and pepper and some garlic.

Keep whisking, never mind reading the book, you'll burn the sauce.

Turn down your sauce to low and drain your noodles (they are almost pawsta now) in your tennis racket (you still haven't bought a colander?). To serve, scoop a big pile of noodles (they are about to be transformed into Pawsta) onto plates and then pour that lovely cheese sauce on top. Yum.

For variety, try cooking some mushrooms in butter and then throwing them in with the sauce, or a couple squirts of ketchup for colour and taste, or even a mug full of chopped fresh tomatoes. Have fun. Yes, now it is Pawsta.

Lemon, Lime and Lager Chicken

The ruins of our capitalist society. I can't believe that I am selling out. Making my Lemon, Lime and Lager Chicken recipe available to the masses. Such are the things that one has to do to cope with our tax system, a mortgage and a son who eats a lot of Pablum.

Chicken is a splendid dish that will leave you (or your guests) dueling for more. You might want to consider cooking up some rice as a side dish and really dazzling your guests with the dessert that follows. Serves four. Bon Appetit a quatre.

Ingredients

4 skinless chicken breasts *(lower fat that way)*

Some marmalade

1 lemon

1 lime

Some lemon juice

Some lime juice *(in one of those fake plastic limes)*

Some beer

(white wine will work too or whatever you have
left over from your last soiree)

Some corn starch

Some sour cream or plain yogurt

(the low fat types work OK here too)

Some salt and pepper and some paprika

(a sprinkle of this and even chicken breasts blush)

Tools

Pyrex pan

Tin foil

Flipper

Sharp knife

Whisk

Directions

Set the oven to 350 F. Remove any excess fat from the chicken using a sharp knife. Lay the chicken breasts into the Pyrex pan bony side down. Pour about 1/4 mug of lemon juice, 1/4 mug of lime juice and 1 mug of beer or white wine into the pan over the chicken. Blob in 4 heaping spoonfuls of marmalade. Sprinkle in some salt and pepper and paprika.

Use a sheet of tin foil to cover the chicken (shiny side toward the chicken). Tuck the foil in around the edges to ensure a good seal. Put the pan in the oven on a rack somewhere near the middle.

Meanwhile, slice up the lemons and limes into wheels about 1/4" thick. Set them aside. When the chicken has baked for about 1/2 hour, carefully remove the tin foil and use a knife to make a small incision in the chicken. If the juice is clear it is done. If the juice is pink and the veins are still visible, give it another five minutes or so.

Use a spoon to spread some more marmalade over the chicken, remove the foil and set the oven control to broil. Slide the pan back in and let it broil for about 4 minutes with the rack set so that the tops of the chicken are about 6" from the element.

At this point you wouldn't want to answer the phone or the smoke alarms may go off.

Pull it out again, lay the lemon and lime slices over the chicken and add a tad more marmalade onto the slices just to shine them up. Slide the works back into the oven for about another 2 minutes.

The secret finishing touch

Pour off the remaining juices from the pan into a glass and skim off any fat. In a mug, mix one heaping spoonful of corn starch with enough cold water to make a paste. Add some sour cream or yogurt to make it totally awesome. Combine the cornstarch paste and the remaining chicken cooking juices in a frying pan on low heat, whisk constantly until it begins to thicken. Don't boil it or it will get lumpy.

Remove the chicken from the Pyrex pan and position nicely on plates with the lemon and lime garnishes. Pour some of the sauce over the chicken. Add a side dish of rice or noodles. Serve with a glass of Dom Perignon, or if budgets are a little tight, you can substitute a glass of no-name Soda water.

Flaming Cointreau Ice Cream

With such a scintillating entrée, only an equally dramatic dessert would be fitting. Few can match the simplicity, elegance and gourmet flair of this delightful offering.

Ingredients

Some Cointreau or virtually any liqueur that
you have around or can borrow
Some French Vanilla Ice Cream or virtually
any kind you have lying around

Tools
Frying pan

Matches

(Borrow some. Always a great way to meet the neighbours)

Fire Extinguisher

Directions

Scoop some ice cream into each serving dish. Wet your spoon between scoops. Distribute the ice cream in dishes to your guests. Pour about 1/2 mug of Cointreau into the frying pan and heat over a low burner until you are overcome with fumes. After dimming the lights, light a match over (not into, or the liquid will dowse the flame) the heated Cointreau and pour the flaming booze over the ice cream. Enjoy at once. Asbestos gloves optional, fire insurance recommended.

Fancy-Lillie-Heidebrecht Cheesecake

Oops. You were making a Flaming Cointreau Ice Cream dessert. Things got a little out of hand. The match struck, the tablecloth went up and your date ended up with a pair of singed eyebrows. The relationship came to a screeching halt.

You are now most interested in a safe dessert with a minimal chance of medical complications during creation or consumption. For you, allow me to recommend the Fancy-Lillie-Heidebrecht Cheesecake. This fine dessert is named after its Bay Street inventors who used this very dessert to sweeten both their initial offering as well as their detailed prospectus and have now progressed to a happy and successful merger. All the best Mark and Karen!

After getting the recipe from them, Ann Heidebrecht offered some time-saving tips to make it even easier. It is really the Fancy-Lillie Cheesecake with a Heidebrecht Hybrid, but whatever, it tastes great and you don't even have to bake the thing.

Ingredients
For the crust
2 mugs of crushed chocolate Graham crumbs
or vanilla wafers
1/4 mug of sugar
1/2 mug of melted butter

For the filling
2 packages of Philadelphia Cream Cheese
1 big tub of Cool Whip
1/2 mug of sugar
1 spoon of lemon juice
2 mugs of fruit
(blueberries, raspberries, chopped kiwis
or whatever you've got)

Tools

Either your 8"x 8" Pyrex pan or see if you can
borrow a spring form pan from someone.
*(They are round aluminum things that look like
something that was discarded from the Space Shuttle
or some sort of primitive torture device.
You will know one when you see one.)*
Small pot
Electric beaters or a blender
*(If you don't have, borrow from your neighbour.
You could end up as happy as the
Tasters Choice couple on TV)*
Mixing bowl

Directions

Heat up your butter in the small pot or just leave it on
your window sill or balcony in a bowl if it is hot outside.
With your butter melted, just mush together all of the
crust ingredients listed above. Press them into your pan
about 1/4 inch deep or about 60% of a centimetre for all
you metric fans. Presto! The crust is done.

For the filling, let your cream cheese warm up to room
temperature or give it a blast in your microwave it you
have one. Put the cream cheese and the Cool Whip into
your Mixing Bowl. Use your blender or electric beaters
on low speed to blend the cream cheese with the Cool
Whip.

By now you probably have a white Cool Whip beard and look like Santa and you will be picking bits of cream cheese off the ceiling for months. No matter. Persevere. Re-read the section on goals in the time management chapter.

With the Cool Whip and the cream cheese all mixed in together, add in the sugar and the lemon juice. Clean off your beaters and put them away. Dump in your fruit and mix it in with a spoon. Easy now. Scrape the whole mixture out of the bowl and onto your crust that has been patiently waiting in its pan.

Smooth out the top so that it is level. (Use a ruler, the edge of your calculator, or in a pinch, your hand). Stick the whole works in the fridge for 4 hours or so and serve.

A Parting Word

You found some great food, cheap and quick and incidentally good. And just as promised, you also found a few tricks to take care of evil food gobbling roommates. Further, you found ways to cook and eat that gently advanced you to newer gastronomic heights.

You are now ready to impress anyone. Everyone.

But a parting word while you still have that borrowed blender in your possession. You gotta try my

Secret Power Breakfast

Take the top off the blender and plop in a peeled banana, a half mug of orange juice and a half mug of plain low fat yogurt. Fit the cover back on and give it a buzz just till it all looks smooth and creamy.

Guzzle it down and you are set for the day. Tell the folks about your nourishing breakfast and what do you want to bet is your present for your birthday?

Thanks to all who shared their recipes. Got a student delicacy that I haven't covered? Send it along to the publisher and we'll get it in next time.

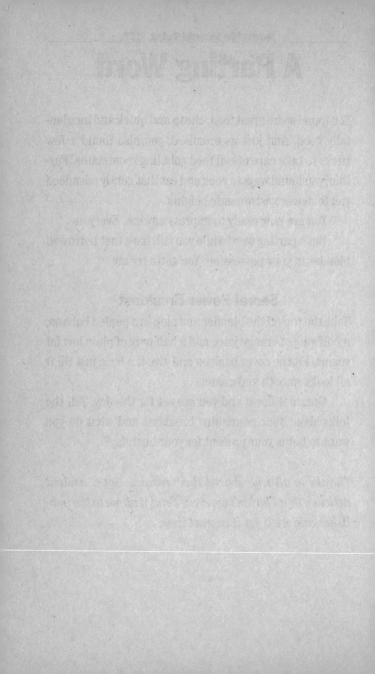

CHAPTER
4

=

Fighting Student Stress and Spread

=

Workin' it all out

Stumbling in from the cab, you see flashes of stairs, wallpaper and a handrail.

Top of the stairs.

A sharp spin to the right down the hall, into your room. Your jacket falls to the floor. Peeling off your T-shirt, you land face up on the bed. You feel yourself slowly sinking into a soft stillness. And then oblivion.

You float upward through the inky black. A tightness clutches your throat. Dryness. Your tongue is huge and it scratches from side to side. Beads of sweat begin to form on your forehead, trickling over your eyebrows. Your throat constricts further. Lights throb through the window from the street below as the room begins a slow motion spin.

Your hands grip the sheets to steady the ride. A chill rushes through your body. The spins continue. Lifting your head from the pillow makes it all worse. Your blood rushes from one end to the other like you are on an unseen roller coaster. A powerful wave of nausea grips your stomach and seizes in on your throat. There is no escape.

You feel gross.

Suddenly, something twists in your stomach. Too much beer. A leap from the bed and a dash down the hall. A flip of the switch and the slam of the lid upward. The dull thud as your knees hit the bathroom floor. There's a flood upward out of your throat and even through your nostrils. A barrage of Aarrrrggghhh. Another wave of last evening's indulgences blows out of your mouth in reverse order of its entrance just a few short hours ago.

How did that work again in accounting class? Was it last in first out or first in first or – Aarrrrggghhh! More evidence of last evening's excesses splash into the bowl. As the tears stream from your bloodshot eyes, you rise to your feet and twirl open the sink faucets. A few cold splashes on your face and a solid brushing of the world's most awful tasting teeth make a world of difference.

You stumble back and sit on the edge of your bed, gazing down aimlessly at that disgusting gut that has been expanding since the start of school. In between the stresses of classes, this term has been a tapestry of late nights, beer, overdue assignments, nachos, tequila, pizzas, residence food and hangovers. Your concentration has fallen off, your marks are down and you look like hell.

Aside from the one daily sit-up necessary to get out of bed, exercise is only a foggy memory.

Wait. There must be some activity that you have been involved in lately. Wasn't there a baseball game a few weeks ago? Oh yeah. It was one that you had watched on the TV at a buddy's place. Nope. No exercise. Ugh. Ugh Aarrgggghhhhh. Another convulsion sends you sprinting down the hall...

Your Belt Needn't Expand with Your Knowledge

Most students start off their school years with the elaborate rituals of an orientation program. Generally these programs are a lot of fun, a great way to meet the rest of your class and a recipe for exhaustion. Screeching endless choruses of school songs, parading around in sweat soaked T-shirts and consuming immense quantities of whatever is on tap, can burn out even the most diehard student party animal.

What too many students forget is that initiation period does have an ending.

There will come a time when you will realize that the back to back parties will have to yield to a more balanced lifestyle permitting you to get through your program so that you will be able to graduate still fitting into the clothing that you arrived on campus with.

One of the key components of a happy healthy lifestyle involves getting a little exercise. Ahh yes - the 'E' word. I know. Sounds like a lot of hard work. You'd rather wolf down a bag of double chocolate Oreos and watch Unsolved Mysteries. Right? Well, like it or not, watching TV and eating cookies won't get you in better shape – uh, did you say double chocolate?

Gimme that bag.

Getting started is the toughest

No choice, you gotta do it.

If you have any history of health problems begin with a trip to your doctor to make sure that your new, and likely over-zealous exercise program won't cause you to blow a gasket, buckle your knees or free up some slimy piece of crud in your arteries to aimlessly drift into a critical area and shut down some important function that you would prefer to maintain in operating condition.

Be sure to tell the doctor that you have seen the evils of your slothful ways and you are about to embark on a new era of healthful eating and invigorating work outs. Find out if she has any reservations or concerns with this type of approach. Is your heart and cardiovascular system sound? Do you have any inherent problems with any of your joints or limbs? What about other problems that may be lurking in your carcass? All clear? Great.

If not, follow your doctor's warning and sit on the side lines for any activities not recommended. Before heading out, ask your doctor to recommend a dietitian for some information on food and nutrition to complement your new exercise program. No doctor or dietitian? Go and see the health services office at your school. You already know the old saw about prevention being better than a cure.

Workouts put it all in perspective

Why are we trying to get fit?

The stats are awesome. Fitness can help prolong your life span, give you additional energy, reduce the chance of injury in everyday life and even the severity of some illnesses, bolster your self esteem, improve your capacity for sports and activities, finely chisel your whole body to make everyone hot for you and give you that very specific wonderful feeling that the French call "Je ne sait quoi." (Forgot your grade ten French? Look it up!)

All that and it has a special way of wiping out tension, anxiety and stress. Whether you are feeling loggy or tense, or even just worried, working out puts it all into perspective.

What should I wear?

Next step is to get yourself some proper footwear and comfortable workout clothing. Shoes can be very important since the wrong ones can result in sore feet, sore knees or simply ugly shoes. Cross trainers can be a good compromise for everything except long distance running or jogging where you will want something with some extra cushioning.

If your activity of interest is likely to be running, spend some extra time (and money) to have a shoe fitter at a specialty sports store examine your feet, gait and running style since proper running shoes are essential to get the right mix of comfort, control and cushioning.

Head down to the recreation facility on your campus. Same problem as when I told you to go to the library, right? Well, if you can't find it, try getting a map of the campus or asking someone. Dating tip here: don't ask a member of the opposite sex where the gym is. Especially if it's half way through the school year. Also, before you ask someone for directions for the gym, make sure you have concealed your problem areas. Guys – suck in that gut, or cover it with a jacket. Girls – try that sloppy sweater look, or go for a pair of baggy sweat pants to keep those saddlebags in check.

When you do arrive at the recreation area, get some brochures to learn about the facilities. Usually, for a small extra fee, you will be able to join the recreation complex and take advantage of all the facilities. Note their hours of operation so that you can plan your workouts around your class schedule. You will need to work on a number of different areas of fitness, so with all of the literature of the recreation area in hand, it's time to build your own fitness plan.

The Elements of Fitness

Strength

Many of you may make the mistake of confusing strength and fitness. Strength is an important component of fitness, but it is by no means the complete picture. A brick wall may possess immense strength, but it would have considerable difficulty keeping up with you on even a lethargic day.

Strength is determined by the ability of a muscle to contract against a load. The more powerful the contraction, the greater the capability of the muscle to move the load. Strength can be increased through the overload principle, that is, repeatedly working a muscle beyond its capacity will cause it to strengthen.

Take it easy for the first month to avoid injuries and always include solid warm-up, stretch and cool down elements to your program. Also be sure to work weights slowly since maximum benefit is attained by working the muscle carefully in each direction. Expert advice and demonstrations are usually there for the asking.

Flexibility

Ever see one of those Neanderthal types circling around the beach holding their arms out from their sides? What gives? Sunburned arm pits? Could be. Maybe just not enough stretching.

While improving strength gives you a feeling of confidence and power, improving your flexibility can reduce aches and pains and give your body a wonderful sense of fluidity. To improve your flexibility, you'll want to stretch your major muscle groups gently to gradually lengthen them, giving you freedom of movement and relief from stiffness.

Cardiovascular fitness

Ever notice the people on those margarine commercials outside in the sunshine, gardening, jogging and cycling? How come no one is out of breath? They didn't get that way from eating margarine. Even the best margarine.

Same story on those beer commercials. While a cooler full of beer may help to get the party started around your beach blanket, it won't get you to the Frisbee any faster. Most of us probably wouldn't last through 30 seconds of beer-commercial-level-activity. We would start out playing a little beach volleyball and by the 20 second mark, collapse face down, huffin', puffin' and spitting out tiny grains of sand while those fit imported stunt people finish up the match.

Cardiovascular fitness is the overall efficiency of the heart and the lungs as well as the myriad of plumbing that distributes all of the little goodies throughout your body. The key is to get in at least three good workouts of twenty minutes or more each week to elevate your heart rate. This will help you to improve the whole system, top to bottom.

Body composition

If you have been taping packages of hot dogs to your stomach to get that 'washboard look' this is the section for you. Body composition deals with the relative percentage of fat in your body. Like everything else, keeping your percentage of body fat to a reasonable level is an onerous task. It also gets a little tougher each year.

Expensive gyms are capable of actually measuring your percentage of body fat, but as students we will have to resort to less expensive means. Try a full length mirror. Guys, start with the profile view. Carrying a bit of a paunch? How about the head-on view? Are those little love handles we see around that waist?

OK you girls. Stop laughing and get in front of that mirror. Oops. Heading out to the Sierra Nevada to meet Clint Eastwood? No? Well then, you won't be needing those saddlebags.

Try lifting an arm and putting one hand near your head. Give it a bit of a shake. Does the back of your arm jiggle just like your grade three teacher's did when she wore one of those sleeveless dresses and wrote something near the top of the chalkboard?

You get the picture. By stepping up some exercise and eating less junk food, we can firm up all of those nasty excesses. Then we won't have to avoid mirrors or wince when they catch us.

And while we are still on the subject of body composition, don't forget that most of it is water. Can't beat a glug of cold water, before, during and after your workouts. Special glucose drinks? For most of our efforts, plain water is still the best.

Building the Plan

Begin by figuring out which activities you think that you might enjoy doing. For strength you will have to rely on some weight training, for flexibility you will need to do some stretching, but to improve your body composition and to heighten your cardiovascular fitness, you can do anything that will get you breathing hard.

The answer to that smirk and the question that you just had is yes, provided that you can regularly do it for twenty minutes at a time, three times a week. Right. Ideally, you should combine several cardiovascular activities to give you some variety. Besides, you need to work some different muscle groups.

The following sections will lay out some details on each of the main areas of Warm-Up, Stretching, Cardiovascular and Strength training. Each of your exercise sessions should begin with five to ten minutes of warm-up to get things moving. Work in a brief stretching period and then move into your focus area, usually either a strength or cardiovascular session, or both. Always end with a complete stretching session to avoid stiffness and possible injury.

Warming Up

Prior to doing vigorous activities like the cardiovascular ones below, drink some water and then spend five minutes or so doing some slow, large body movements to get all of the juices flowing in the joints. Try some jogging on the spot, some large swirling movements of the arms and some gentle bending of the spine.

With the juices flowing and the muscles lightly warmed up, it's time to get in some stretching. With all stretches, the key is to do them slowly without jerking or straining. Begin the stretch and move the limb to the point where it just begins to meet with some resistance. Hold it there for ten seconds and then try to stretch it just a little further for another ten seconds. Release and move on to the next stretch.

Stretching

Neck

Work in a stretch to one side by slowly easing your head on your shoulder and then gently lift and ease it to the other shoulder. Finish up by holding your shoulders firm and then turning your head all the way to the left, hold and then to the right. Do not roll the head in a circle or you will hear all manner of crunching noises as you lay the foundation for an 'Igor-like' posture in your later years.

Arms

Stand with your one arm perpendicular to your torso and your body facing a wall. Press the whole length of the extended arm against the wall and rotate your body away, stretching the area where your arm joins in to your chest. Hold, and then try the other arm.

Use one arm to hold the opposite elbow and pull the other arm straight across the chest until you feel the pull

in your upper arm. Hold. Do the other side.

Reach behind your head with your right hand and touch your left shoulder. Use your left hand to reach up and grab your right elbow, gently pulling it downward and to your left. This is a great one for loosening up before

and after racquet sports. (It is also great to pull out a few kinks when you've been studying for hours. Try it in the library and pretty soon everyone will be doing it. Except maybe the librarian.) Hold and enjoy the stretch. Don't forget to do the other side.

Backs

Backs are so controversial that I won't even tell you how to stretch your back for fear of lawsuits, mountains of letters from physical therapists and doctors and scores of paralyzed readers in traction. Ask your doctor or a qualified attendant at the gym to give you some stretches for your back.

Legs
Front of thighs

Lift your right heel up towards your buttocks. Reach around behind your back and grab your right foot with your left hand, pulling it up and away from your back. Keep about a foot of space between your foot and your buttocks. Hold. Try adding a little extra pull and then holding for another ten seconds or so. Oh yeah. Don't forget to keep your balance. Might help to hang on to the wall or a chair or something. Do the other side.

Back of thighs (hamstrings)

If you don't stretch anything else, be sure to stretch these little babies. Pulled hamstrings are very common, painful and slow to heal. To stretch 'em without hurting anything else, lay on your back, raise your right leg and grab your leg with both hands, just behind the knee. Slowly straighten your right leg by maintaining your grip and raising your right foot. Hold. Try to raise the straightened leg a little further. Hold. Do the other side.

Front of Calves

Standing straight, cross your right foot over your left, pointing your toes so that your right toe is touching the ground near the outside of your left heel. By bending your

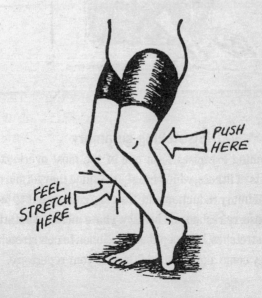

PUSH
HERE

FEEL
STRETCH
HERE

left knee you will be able to push on the back of your right calf, stretching the muscle along the front of your right shin. Hold. Do the other side.

Back of Calves

Stand facing a wall. Lean forward and place your palms against the wall with your feet on the floor. Make small steps backward and press your feet flat against the floor until you feel a stretch along the back of your calves. Hold.

Stretching summary

Stretching exercises form one of the most overlooked aspects of fitness, which is a shame since they form a big part of injury reduction and are a key component to feeling loose, refreshed and healthy. I have included a starter kit of stretches, but keep your mind open to new stretches as they come along and add them to your repertoire.

Good aerobics classes that are led by certified instructors are an excellent place to 'steal' some new stretching ideas. Be sure to stretch before and after exercise, but especially afterwards. Also, never stretch a cold muscle — always begin with at least five minutes of warm up.

Cardiovascular or Aerobic Conditioning

The Cardio portion of your workout is perhaps the most important from a perspective of health and a general sense of well being. Cardio workouts include all those that pick up the pace of breathing (not just faster but also deeper) and pulse rate, giving the whole heart and blood system a what for. It provides an essential relief of stress which in practical terms means being able to concentrate deeply and to sleep soundly. But not at the same time.

For cardiovascular exercise, there are a myriad of choices including: swimming, running, jogging, fast walking, aerobics classes, tennis, squash, badminton, bicycling, rowing, touch football, soccer, basketball, cross-country skiing or hiking. The best of these involve a continuous effort and ideally, do not put excessive stress on your joints.

It's not a bad idea to start with some lower impact events like fast walking or swimming and move up to higher impact events like running or squash if they interest you. Picking activities that are competitive will generally take your mind off the exertion and will result in a program that is more fun and easier to stick with.

A good cardiovascular program might include a run on Monday evenings before the Physics Class, a half hour swim Wednesday before Melrose Place, a regular lunch hour squash game with Cindy on Thursdays and a pick up game of touch football or basketball with the gang on Sunday afternoon. Each of the events in the sample is good for improving cardiovascular fitness, provided you keep the activity sustained throughout the period. And take along a bottle of plain water.

Checking out the pulse

In each cardiovascular workout, you will want to get your heart rate up to about 150 to 170 beats per minute. That equates to 25 to 28 beats in 10 seconds. (Your actual maximum heart rate is about 220 beats per minute minus your age, and you should aim to exercise at about 80% of that number).

To take your pulse, place your index and middle fingers of your right hand on the outer edge of the 'Adam's Apple' on your throat. Feel around and you should feel a pulsing at your fingertips. Try doing some exercise and note how it picks up the pace. Get used to what a rate of 150 to 170 beats per minute feels like so that you won't have to sink to the bottom of the pool or interrupt a basketball game to check it out.

If it suits your style, you may want to involve yourself in a little competition to keep your routine going, reduce boredom and add an additional sense of satisfaction. For example, if you enjoy running, why not try entering some 10K races, or if you enjoy squash, sign up on a squash ladder. Knowing that you have a game booked with someone or that there is a race coming up is a great way to stay motivated and enthused about your cardio workouts.

Strengthening Exercises

Improving muscular strength is important for both men and women. Strengthening exercises are best done in a properly equipped gym. Most schools have excellent strength training facilities available right on campus. I will outline a few of the basic strength exercises using weights to build and tone the major muscle groups. Before plunging into these strength exercises, be sure to do the warm up and stretch moves.

If you are unfamiliar with how to adjust the weights or how to use the specific apparatus in the gym, ask one of the staff for some assistance before dropping something on your toe. Always begin with a light load that you can comfortably manage before working up, especially on your first trip to the gym.

In all weight exercises move smoothly and slowly using only the muscle being exercised, exhaling as you exert yourself and inhaling as you return to the starting position. If, for whatever reason, you prefer to exercise without using weights, we will look at some other exercises that will perform a similar role without the use of weights.

There are dozens of different exercises that you can do to build strength with or without weights. I will outline a few of the simpler ones that will get you started. Always begin your new program with a weight that you are comfortable with, gradually building to a more intense workout with heavier weights and more repetitions over time.

Generally, aim for a weight with which you can comfortably perform ten repetitions. Each group of repetitions is called a set. Take thirty to sixty second breaks between sets to give your muscles a chance to re-group and then hit 'em with another set or two.

The Bench Press

This is a good general strength exercise that will build strength in the upper chest and the back of the upper arms. Lie on your back on the bench press apparatus. The weight bar should be directly above your shoulders for balance. Press the weight away from your chest until your arms are fully extended and then lower the weight back down to your chest.

Repeat ten times, rest for sixty seconds and then do another 10 repetitions. If you are starting out or moving up to a heavier weight and are using 'free' weights (not part of a machine), have someone spot you to make sure you don't crush your rib cage.

To work the same muscles without weights, try doing push ups. Keep your back straight and your arms shoulder width apart. Lower yourself until your nose touches the ground and then push up until your arms are extended. To work your chest more, try moving your arms further apart. To build your arms try doing some with your thumbs touching.

The Arm Curl

If you crave a set of biceps like Arnold's this is the exercise for you. Beginning with your arms at your side and the weights in your hands, exhale as you raise your forearms, keeping everything else perfectly still. Don't jerk your back. Continue moving very slowly and deliberately for ten repetitions. Rest for sixty seconds and do ten more.

Without weights, you can do chin ups, if your gym has a chinning bar. Try working with an underhand grip and work your way up to two or three sets of ten. For variety and to work different muscles, try overhand grips and wider grip. Between Bench Presses and Curls you have built a solid foundation toward upper body and arm strength.

The Sit-up

Long the staple of choleric, stern-faced grade ten gym teachers, sit-ups carry a negative stigma. Like artichokes and escargot, sit-ups are definitely an acquired taste. Give them time and your concentrated effort and they will reward you with a powerful washboard worthy of your suntan oil. Neglect your sit-ups and you will invite poor posture, back pain and a flaccid gut that will congregate in heaving rolls of pink flesh.

To work the upper 'abs', try lying on your back, knees bent and apart, with your hands touching your ears and your elbows out. Focus on using your stomach muscles to raise your chin to the ceiling or as close as you can get it. (Apparently Brian Mulroney and Jay Leno were a little overzealous on this one during their college days). Feel the tightening? Love it. Tune and tighten that tubby tummy. Hold it at the top for half a second, then ease back down, inhaling as you go. Speed is not the point here, concentrated focused effort is the way to go.

How many should you do? I don't know. You can do more than you think. Go easy for the first month or so to get your body used to the whole thing. Then do enough so that you definitely feel it. When you reach a point where you begin to communicate with Your Maker under your breath, squeeze out about five more.

Relax for a few seconds, then get in another set. Stomach doesn't look much different after two weeks? Be patient. Rome wasn't built in a day and it has taken you your whole life to cultivate that curvaceous gut. Give it a chance. But keep that flat vision in the mind.

Now, for the lower abs. This one is especially important for the ladies. Jeans getting a little tight? Lay off the Pop Tarts and the crackers for a while as you terrorize your stomach into submission. Lie on your back , knees bent and apart while settling your feet flat on the floor. Keeping your hands cupped behind your ears, think stomach as you slowly lift and aim your elbow to the opposite knee. Hold a few seconds then ease back down, this time keeping your head just a bit above the floor.

Start with five or so to each knee and increase gradually to more. Keep your mind on that flat midriff, firm waist and abs that will soon be yours. Feel those lower stomach muscles? Did you ever get the thrill of feeling them before? Got that image of what you are working for? Sneak in five more. Enjoy.

Leg Exercises

There are a host of different exercises that you can do, but if you have built yourself a good cardiovascular program with workouts that involve leg muscles such as running, swimming or cycling, you will probably get in all of the leg strengthening that you will need. If you do want to use some weights on your legs, get some instruction from the gym supervisor so that you don't damage your knees.

Finishing Your Workout

Do some final stretches to cool down , slug down some cool water and then head for the shower. If you don't finish off with some stretching, you are likely to be stiff for the next few days. If your facility has a steam room or a sauna, even better. Get in five minutes worth, shower and get changed. Tomorrow, aside from a few stretches to keep things loose and easy, take the day off.

Keep at it , it pays off

Fitness is a must to feel and look your best. Keeping a regular program of fitness going takes incredible mental toughness. It's worth it. That discipline and pride in yourself seeps over into other activities as well. Build a plan that you can live with, by incorporating activities that you enjoy.

No one has the mental stamina to ride a stationary bike for twenty minutes at a time over a span of forty years.

If nothing else, get in some good cardiovascular exercise on a regular basis. It will give you unbelievable energy and keep you feeling refreshed. Stress and spread won't be on your list of worries. It will also help you to build a great habit that will keep you off the operating table in your later years.

Good luck!

CHAPTER

5

=

Examining the Student Body

=

Steps to dynamic dating

It had been over three months since your last date.

All the bad signs were there. Some 'helpful' friends had assembled a support group for you. Hours of (slightly biased) personal scrutiny in the mirror had failed to yield any clues as to the reasons for your monk-like existence. Your Dad had begun to offer some of the techniques that he used to use to get dates when he was in school. Your Mom had placed a call to her Aunt Verda in Spokane to see if her friend Lois' daughter Bessie was interested in coming up to meet you.

The situation had grown desperate.

Like a cruise missile, friend's conversations seemed to be precision-guided to your failures in dating. An impromptu gathering in the gym locker room quickly turned to an unrequested brain storming session.

"How about Sue?" offered Mark.

"Too smart – she'd have him figured out in a second," quipped Greg, before you could offer your acceptance of the idea.

"We need someone who could relate to a dull guy. Someone not too focused on looks either," suggested Ken.

"No woman is that desperate," shot back Mark, intent on dousing the last remaining flicker of your ego.

"False advertising," offered Greg to a roomful of blank stares including yours.

"False advertising. We'll run an ad in the personal column of the student paper. We'll build him up a bit. By the time she figures out what she's really in for, they'll be on a date. Mission accomplished." Greg sat back with a look of satisfaction having delivered his plum idea.

"You guys are going to advertise me?" you ask.

"OK, let's do it," came the group response to what was meant as a rhetoric question.

The gang promised to get back with the final copy before placing the ad in the newspaper. Two days later, you catch up with Mark on campus. He flashes a big grin before passing you the typed final copy:

Tall, intellectual yet sensitive and conshientious guy, 21, with broad shoulders, wing tips, button downs and Polo After Shave seeks fun loving gal, 20-25 with sports car and trust fund to share quiet evenings, strolling through art galleries, enjoying philosophical discussions and Nietzsche readings. Reply Box 125.

"Nietzsche readings? What is Nietzsche readings?" you ask in disbelief.

"Don't worry, it's intellectual. Women love that stuff," assured Mark, perhaps your least trustworthy friend; a guy who has spent far more hours in front of his PC that in front of women.

"You spelled conscientious wrong."

"Women love to correct men, they need to find something to change."

"What's this about a trust fund?"

"Read the newspaper. With the job market the way it is you'll want a little extra support. Best to be up front with these things. Trust me."

"OK, OK. But when did I become sensitive?"

"Think sales, sometimes you have to stretch things a bit to get the order. By the way, the ad was forty six bucks. Any chance you can pay me back by Monday? Stick a cheque in my locker. Gotta run –"

"Well, I think we will need to tone it down a – forty six bucks? Don't tell me you've sent it in?"

"Of course, had to get it in quickly before all the best ones are gone. Time kills all dates. Gotta run."

Mark dashed off into the sea of knapsacks, students and bicycles. Oh boy, you think as you ponder the prospects of sifting through dozens of letters written by rich, sensitive, Polo-sniffing, Nietzsche-reading girls desperate to meet Mr. Conshientious.

As the days went on, you wondered how your buddies could get so excited about such nonsense. Talk about childish pursuits. Imagine actually dating someone from a personal ad. What kind of friends would subject a guy to this kind of social roulette?

Unable to stand it, your outer, carefree veneer removed, you race down to the student paper offices and sheepishly quote your box number.

"You must be Box 125," belted out the clerk to the assembled crowd, "You only got one response to your personal ad. Here it is."

Red-faced, you snatch the envelope from her hands and press out past the delighted crowd. Finding a secluded tree, you lean against the sturdy trunk and carefully finger the envelope.

It was a rich parchment paper with your box number typed on the front. You quickly scan around the tree trunk before sniffing the envelope for perfume. Maybe she wears Lady Polo?

Nope, no scent.

What kind of woman is about to revealed? Perhaps tall and exotic, with stories of far away places? Maybe a dark, brown-eyed lady with a biting wit, who just happens to love curling up to watch NFL games? Maybe a short pert blonde, an English major with great skills in analytical essays who would love to ghost write yours?

You can feel an unfamiliar tightness in your throat and you're surprised to see the paper shaking. Must be the wind. Whoa, maybe a saucy redhead with... The wind subsides and the paper unfolds.

"Dear Box 125," [the letter began,] "I enjoyed reading your ad in the paper. Sounds like you possess some interesting qualities ..."

You can't believe that anyone would find the qualities in that ad interesting.

"... While I am afraid that I can't help you with your dating problems, I am a great fan of the works of Mr. Nietzsche. I have a number of his earlier volumes and I am looking for one or two books to complete my set. If you would be interested in making some trades, please let me know. Good luck with your ad, if you get too busy and have some extra replies that you can't handle, let me know. Hope to talk to you soon.

Sincerely,

Jason Roberts

(426) 929-3427.

"Extra replies. Lady Polo. Trust fund." You mutter under your breath. It's going to be a long cold winter.

Tip-toeing through the minefields

With the collective consciousness of North America into some sort of political-correctness-on-steroids, writing a chapter on dating is a bit like tip-toeing through a minefield. My bet is that there will be something in here that will offend virtually everyone. The amusing part is that five years ago, the identical material would have offended virtually no one.

To begin, I will lay down some key assumptions that we will work with throughout the chapter:

1. However tenuous a beginning, and whatever any relationship between two people may develop into, it is a truism that it likely began with some sort of physical attraction and grew from there. Let's work with the crazy notion that since Adam and Eve, men and women still look at each other from across a crowded room (or garden) and something clicks.

2. There exists no ideal term for female-type people. Chicks or babes sends the feminists into orbit. Women sounds a little too matronly. Females is straight from Biology class. Girls sends the feminists back into orbit once again and Gals is too much of a throwback to a 60's Rogers and Hammerstein musical. I will use a mix of terms to try to appease (or aggravate) everyone on an equal footing.

3. With the tremendous epidemic of AIDS and STDs in place, anything beyond a peck on the cheek is getting

dangerous. If things heat up as a result of these dating ideas, be sure to wrap you and your partner in multiple layers of plastic, latex, tin foil or rubber to keep things safe. For a more rigorous treatise on safe sex, pick up a pamphlet at your student health services office on campus. But do more than just pick it up.

4. Although there are numerous other combinations, I will focus on male-female, boy-girl, man-woman, chick-hunk types of relationships. Those of you into other combinations will have to consult with alternate forms of literature for advice. If any of the following ideas works for you anyway, great.

The Dating Guide

This chapter is divided into three sections. The first offers some juicy nuggets for you guys out there on how to attract a really steamy babe (never call 'em babes), the second part of the chapter (written mostly by my wife) offers tips for you female types to land the teddy bear of your dreams (never call 'em teddy bears) and then the third part offers some ideas on how to impress your new catch on a student budget.

If you women out there are upset about the term babes, how do you think we feel about teddy bears? The ideas in here should be suitable for most of you. If you aren't big on dating, re-read the chapter on studying for exams. Or spoon out that tub of ice cream to the cardboard bottom.

Where to Find the Chicks

Naturally, to the get the whole process working, you will need to position yourself in the areas where women tend to congregate. Remember too, that these same women will be assessing your character by what you were doing in the place that they met you.

Of course the flip side is that if they saw you somewhere, you may be able to see them there too and assess their character by their choice of locale. On the other hand, maybe you are both there because you thought that the other one might be there as well. I dunno. Herewith, a list of potential hot spots, the type of girls typically available there and the impression you make by hanging around.

The Laundromat

Cool. Set yourself up as the independent type. No mama's boy here. Get a small box of Tide (big boxes reek of economy) and some unscented Bounce sheets for the dryer. Black T-shirt, faded jeans. Vintage Nicholson. Lose the cigarettes though. Passé. Practice till you get the look right: a touch sensitive, but with a hint of danger. They'll love you.

Bring a magazine to read, adds to the nonchalant

look. Something trendy and ideally, foreign or intellectual. Try Vanity Fair, Paris Match or Architectural Digest.
You want them to head back to the dorm and coo about
your complexity to their roommates.

Now here's the key. A touch of helplessness. Women
can't stand to see whites going in with colours. Leave out
the fabric softener and they will be all over you. Dial in
the wrong temperature rinse and you'll work them up to
a frenzy.

When they finally rush over to help, hit them with an
intense stare. Try a little Tom Cruise from *Top Gun* or
Paul Newman from *Cool Hand Luke*. Or go for some Kevin
Costner from *Field of Dreams*. Beautiful.

The Gymnasium

Well rounded. Self Assured. Scope out a few of the aerobics
classes to find the ones requiring minimal coordination
with the hottest selection of babes (oops). Memorize a
few of the moves and practice up ahead of time at home
and in front of the biggest mirror you can find, so that
you can appear natural. Head back to the gym practiced
up and ready to go. Slide into a spot on the floor next to
the woman of your dreams. Try to appear reasonably fluid,
but be careful not to be too good.

By doing lunges in the opposite direction to your prospective wife, you will be able to get some eye contact
going. Work through the moves and pretend to enjoy the
music. However nubile and sinewy the crowd, don't stare.

If you were cheating and couldn't do the exercises, bring along a spray bottle of water and give yourself a few good sprays in the face and chest. As the class applauds itself, saunter over and ask if you can buy her a mineral water and some carrot sticks. Dynamite.

The Car Repair Shop

Like men, women need to get their cars fixed too. Often they will be in a sullen mood, awaiting an exorbitant bill to change some greasy car part that evidently is holding them up from going about their business.

Naturally, you can tune your audience by selecting the type of repair shop to hang out at. A place that specializes in old VW campers would be great if you are looking for a 60's throwback, artsy type who likes to go camping on the weekends and paints pastoral scenes using natural-based paints and bulrushes for brushes.

If you are looking for a slick uptown girl, try ambling around the Porsche dealership. If you want to get married and have kids right away, go straight to the Volvo dealer and wear one of those baby snugglies. Borrow a friend's kid if you have to. Listen in when she speaks with the mechanic to catch a bit of the terminology. Leaving your four-hour-old BMW key fob hanging from your sweaty palm, approach the coachless lass and deliver your line.

"Control Pressure Regulator gone? Darn Bimmers. I make a great Bluefish Fettucini. (Toss in some little slices of grilled bluefish with the KD). How about dinner next week?"

The only person in the world sensitive to her problems has just asked her out to dinner. Don't forget your "Haute de Cuisine" recipes. Bon Appetit.

The Cafeteria

The salad bar. Perfect. Attracts the healthy ones. Do a first pass to memorize the lay out. By sucking in your gut and cruising the salad bar you're likely to look like one of those impossibly healthy types that she's been reading about in Cosmo. Think William Hurt or Mel Gibson. (Try borrowing some of those 'serious' round wire frame glasses from someone).

Position yourself just upstream of that vegetarian vision and wait until her plate is about 2/3 full. Carefully select a ripe leaf of endive and artistically drape it over her tofu.

As your tongs retreat, stare deeply into her eyes and offer, "Tough to get a decent salad around here. Was I too forward with my endive. It just looked right on your plate. I have a class at 1:00, but I can spend a few minutes with you. My table is just over here..."

The Library

Yes, women feign studying just as much as guys. Excellent spot to zero in on some of the artsie types. Superb female density around exam time. Find that beautiful bookworm and scan a few of the titles that she is reading. Ideally, try to pick out the Dewey Decimal numbers. Head to that section of the library and grab two or three

that are within about '20' of the books that she is reading.

Head back to her table and hang your jacket across the back of a chair. As she looks up, get a quick read on her interest level. High degree of annoyance? Pivot on your heel and re-start the procedure somewhere else. Some level of interest? Sit down and do a bit of reading. On the back of a bookmark scribble something about how the beer is warm at the campus pub and you can't concentrate ever since she sat at your table. Remember, home by 11. It's a school night.

Safety First

Two key things here guys: First off, if things pick up some steam bear in mind the legions of microscopic bugs that are lurking out there. These little babies are trying to work their way into your loins where they can wreak havoc with your internal parts and things (see illustration below). Best advice is to put a condom on, put another one on top and then tuck the whole works back in your pants.

Second item is that no means no. If you don't have a signed agreement drawn up by both lawyers, approved in your jurisdiction and notarized by the Supreme Court as well as affidavits and supporting documentation, you are at risk of spending time in the cooler. Move things forward at her speed, not yours.

Where to Find the Hunks

Face it girls, school is the place to track down those elusive Kurt Russell substitutes (and Goldie Hawn already got him). By carefully maneuvering in their habitats, you will be able to woo in the best of them. Use some caution when working in their turf, guys carry a fine line between women who are too fragile (unwilling to toss around a football on the beach) or too butch (popping off beer caps with their teeth). The other approach is to catch them where they are a little off guard. Here are a few places to start...

Big Screen Sports Bars

Check and see if there is one of these bars on campus. Scan the TV listings to find out which sports events are telecast during the week (although Monday Night Football is still a staple). If you aren't up on the sport being televised, do a little reading up or get your Dad or brother to explain it to you. If they grin and ask pressing questions about your sudden interest in football, give them one of those 'pull-eeeezze' stares and a flick of your pony tail.

    With a little knowledge (being a dangerous thing and all) under your belt, head into the bar with a girlfriend and take a position halfway between the screen and the table of your choice. Or take a guy with you and try to stir up some jealous pangs. Order a round of beers for yourselves, but do get glasses. Remember that fine line.

Toss out the odd carefully chosen comment about the game but don't cheer unless you are certain. Use 'uniform' rather than 'outfit', 'touchdown' rather than 'home run' and focus on the athletic accomplishments of the teams rather than the roundness of their butts. At a commercial, casually glance over at the guy who will one day weed your lawn and ask if the score has been flashed on the Cincinnati game.

Touchdown.

The Grocery Store

Aha. There he is, just past the bok choy, squeezing the cantaloupes. How can he not know that cantaloupes are to be sniffed, not squeezed. Men! With your quintessential blunt cut college 'do' swinging, Lauren sweats and Reeboks, you stride over confidently, pausing briefly to gaze at the surface of the meat scale to check your make up.

"I dumped my last boyfriend for that," you toss in nonchalantly, at once piquing his curiosity, demonstrating your current availability, your knowledge of cantaloupe testing and your assertiveness.

"Always sniff a cantaloupe."

Toss a couple of ripe ones into his basket and give him one of those looks like fishing weights are tugging at your eyelids. The heavier the weights, the more likely he is to follow up. If you offer up your number try to look like it wasn't planned.

If you whip out a stack of printed business cards, he will wonder who else's cart you have been tossing cantaloupes into. Better still, get his number or agree to meet somewhere on campus during the day. It is prudent to do some werewolf screening during the daytime hours with all the weirdos out there.

The Squash Ladder

What better way to flash those cellulite-free thighs at the stud of your dreams than to take to the squash court. Sign up on the ladder using a variant of your name that could pass for a man's. Try Billy for Billie, Jack for Jackie or Sam for Samantha. Show up a bit late and head to the viewing area so you can check out the goods on this week's opponent/potential date. If he is a total gweeb, head back to the ladder and switch the match so that he thinks he had the wrong time.

If he fits the bill, smooth your shorts and head down to the court. Maintain just the right mix of competence and helplessness, working your way through to the end of the game. Caution: if you play a strong game, beware the fragile male ego. Or what the hell, whip his ass! Whatever the score, be sure to bet dinner and a movie on it. You can't lose.

The Chemistry Lab

Best locale to select a future doctor with strong anatomy skills. Be sure to wear enough perfume to overpower the paradichlorobenzene. Spend the extra few bucks to get yourself a set of lab glasses that don't leave you looking like something left over from an Addams Family episode. Although you will have to wear a lab coat, who's to be the wiser if you take up the hem a few inches? Position yourself across from the chemist of your choice and set up your flasks and glassware with a studied coolness.

As you begin your titration, gaze through your graduated cylinder and try to meet his glance between the 50cc and 75cc gradations. Try a topical approach, something like "Pass the Carbon Tetrachloride, please". Continue to distill and decant for a while before lowering your glasses slightly and asking him out to compare notes. No catalyst required.

Safety First

If you read the guy's safety first section, you can guess what's coming up here. Unfortunately you do have to be careful to avoid having those same little bugs from hanging out in your uterus or munching on your Fallopian

Tubes. In addition, you likely aren't ready for kids yet. Finally, while you would hope that the guys all act like gentlemen, play it safe.

Don't leave yourself in a situation in the middle of nowhere at night with some hyperactive male hormones zooming in on you. Start things off on double dates and stick to daytime encounters in public places until you are sure that you are safe.

Where to Take 'Em

While most aspects of dating have changed dramatically over the years, the bad news is that the battle still rages over who should pay. On a student budget that can be a painful experience. However, by playing the odds you can avoid looking cheap and save yourself a heap of cash in the interim. The trick is, always be the first to offer to pay. After you offer, pray that an "Oh no, I insist" will come back. Shrug sheepishly and find something to do with your hands as your date whips out the Gold Amex.

Naturally you will need some 'show money' to bluff your way through. Borrow a handful of twenties from a rich friend and flash them around as you offer to pay. No bite? Ouch. You're stuck. Work an extra shift at the campus pub. But it's worth a try.

Whoever pays, you will need to have a few ideas for cheap dates that will enhance your image of Spartan sophistication. Here are five destinations that will advance you to unparalleled popularity.

The Zoo

Ideal as an initial exploratory outing. By closely monitoring your date, you will get an initial pulse on the relationship. Which animals does your date show the most interest in? Any similarities? Hmmm. Note any reaction to those animals with baby animals in the family. In tune with your own?

Does your date have pig-like qualities (eating the stale bread and popcorn rather than feeding it to the zoo residents)? What was the reaction when the baboons began mating? Appalled and disgusted? Intrigued and drew you closer? Salivated and pawed at you frantically? Check your social calendar for next week.

The Drive-In Movie

Ah yes, the drive-in movie.

The romance magnet from our parent's era, where guys and girls went to enjoy a movie, split a Cherry Coke, wolf down bags of buttery popcorn and do some serious frenching and groping. Today, under a thin veil of nostalgia and on a student budget, you can enjoy a movie, split a Diet Pepsi, nibble on some no-salt-no-butter whole wheat popcorn and do some serious frenching and groping. And yes, scary films are still the best. Don't forget the blanket.

The Art Gallery

Best for, you guessed it, the artsie types. As with any other activity, best to do a little prep work so that you view the works right side up. Don't leave your chewing gum wrappers in the statues. Practice the terminology a bit as well: 'Works', not 'paintings'. 'It's a look', rather than 'it sucks'.

"Perhaps one of her earlier pieces", as opposed to, "Was this done by an eight year old?"

"It doesn't assume too much", as an alternative to, "what the hell is it?"

Stare at each piece sagely for about twice as long as it takes to get more than bored with it. A slight nodding of the head and a gentle pursing of the lips will make your date aware that you know art and build the necessary authenticity to make the old line about coming up to see your etchings work.

The Picnic

The venerable old ham and mayo sandwich is transformed into the basis of a romantic renaissance by a checkered tablecloth, a big bottle of cheap wine and a dollop of pâté.

Somewhere between the black fly bites and the incessant buzzing of the crickets the relationship is bound to grow, like the soft fuzzy green moss on the cheese that you forgot to inspect ahead of time. Load up on the cheap but impressive stuff: an old candle or two, a couple of kiwis, a bunch of grapes and a baguette.

By slicing some ham into long strips and sprinkling it with Tabasco, you can probably pawn it off as Prosciutto. With your trusty old Elton John tape crooning softly on your ghetto blaster, something akin to love is bound to develop.

All of this works in winter too. Same picnic basket but no bites or buzzing. Stake out a park bench by a frozen river and watch the ducks and Canada Geese squacking and splashing in icy pockets of water. You'll figure out a way to keep warm.

The Athletic Event

Pick an activity where you have some level of skill. Borrow the necessary rock climbing, windsurfing, parachuting, hang gliding or spelunking equipment and head for the best cliff, waves, airport, mountain or cave in the area and have at it.

An old bandanna will help to mop the sweat and some sun screen will help to keep the ozone from breaking down your date's bodily defenses before you do. To avoid being too healthy, mix up the after-event treats a little. A bag of Oreos and a six pack of Bud chilling on ice will show your diversity.

Make sure that you wear your deodorant so that you can both keep the moment fresh and special after you have climbed, sailed, fallen, soared and explored your little hearts out.

Summary

Almost anyone can find a date with a little work and an original approach. Most people have had it with cliché pick up lines and lukewarm follow through. It even helps to pursue activities and events that you genuinely care about, then no matter what the season, genuine passion and sincerity will warm two hearts.

Work in a little sizzle with the steak and enjoy the best dating years of your life. Screaming kids, mountains of bills and burnt toast are just around the corner!

PART TWO

=

LET'S GET SERIOUS

=

Chapter 6: Post Procrastinating
Time management for the rushin' student

Chapter 7: Organized Grime
Papers, laundry and cupboards

Chapter 8: Avoiding Arithmetic Armageddon
Breaking the math barrier

Chapter 9: The Taming of the Verb
Essays and research made easy

Chapter 10: Making the Grade
You too can pass exams

Chapter 11: Creating a Career
Post grad proving ground

=

Post Procrast- inating

=

Time management for the rushin' student

Ten years later. I still have the nightmare.

I am back in engineering school. In the sunny days of September, I am busy purchasing textbooks, racing from class to class, meeting classmates and grasping to understand what each new course is all about. With six subjects competing for my time, days blur into weeks, fade to months and a whole term nearly slips by.

Exams and assignments materialize, are submitted and the dismal results displayed back all too graphically. Friendships grow, romances wax and wane, jeans fade and grunge accumulates on the shelves of my refrigerator. The end of the term nears.

The final scramble to get the last bits of work done begins. Clear the decks for the finals. Old exams are passed around and studied with intensity. Joining the gang in the cafeteria, the discussion turns to the inevitable exam schedule.

The group begins to discuss some of the material for one upcoming exam. Bits of the talk whirl around in my mind, inciting an evil, dreading sense of déja vu. A vague recollection materializes. I seem to be enrolled in a course that I can only vaguely recall. An unbearable pressure descends on my back and shoulders. My heart pounds in my ears and I can't even swallow.

No matter how desperately I try to join in their discussions, I seem to be bodily drifting away, blurred memories swirl elusively. No one seems aware of my dilemma and confusion.

The truth begins to dawn. The exams begin this week, not next. The course exam that they are discussing starts in one hour. I am now only aware that my mouth has dropped itself open.

I haven't been to any of the lectures except the first two back in September. I don't even know why I didn't go. How could I forget about an entire course for a whole term?

I snatch a textbook off the table and desperately flip pages hoping something will magically shoot out from the pages into my coagulated brain and park a while. I inhale deeply, maybe I can somehow draw the knowledge in with my very breath.

But the collage of Greek and English letters, the text, the italics and the numbers swirl in a vortex devoid of meaning. The pages seem to expand and then contract, dizzyingly taunting. This is real. My breathing seems laboured and confused .

Fear has overcome me. My year is destroyed. My future has vapourized.

I wake up.

From Nightmares to Mastery

Poor time management can leave us with a constant feeling of uncertainty that blooms into nightmares like this one. More specifically, we really need to manage the events in our lives, the time will take care of itself.

Much of the stress of school and ultimately the working world is caused by a constant and underlying fear that there exists some event that you should be preparing for, or some item that you have forgotten.

The first step in living a more relaxed lifestyle is to get more closely in sync with what you need to accomplish in the next hour, week, or month and to get a plan in place to tackle it.

Once you have that plan together, rolling it out tends to be the easy part. Onward then to the mastery of our events, and the time they require. After all, it waits for no one.

Daily planners

The best place to begin is with a daily planner to keep track of pub nights, dates, cafeteria specials and yes, even such vestiges as exam schedules and study group meetings.

Step one is to go out and buy yourself a good one. No need to get too fancy. Don't spend a lot of money for one that provides international time zones when the only phone calls you make are to arrange dates and you seldom carry on romances across the international date line. Similarly, a wine chilling chart is a touch redundant if your principal aperitif is a Snapple.

Look for a daily planner that gives ample room for each day and has some blank pages in the front to allow room for your goals and empty sections in the back where you can record little pearls of wisdom as they materialize in your cranium. It is often useful to get one with removable pages so that you can transfer key events from day to day if you couldn't get them accomplished. Pick one large enough for some details, but small enough that you will always keep it with you. Take your new book home and get it set up.

Goals

They may be boring and cliché, but they are essential. What and by when? The four minute mile was not eclipsed because Roger Bannister ambled to the corner store for a quart of Butter Brickle Ice Cream and then elected to see how quickly he could race home with it. Einstein did not develop his theory of relativity while gabbing with friends on the phone, scratching his gut and idly flipping over cards in a game of solitaire. Amelia Earhart didn't get her pilot's license by playing Microsoft Flight Simulator while munching a piece of chocolate babka.

Begin your new journey of event and time mastery by writing out what it is that you hope to accomplish this term. Sounds crazy, but put it in writing. To aid in this exercise, use the following categories as examples to ensure that you are covering all goal areas that are relevant to you:

Scholastic

- What grades do you hope to accomplish in each subject?
- Are you aiming for top quartile overall?
- Dean's List?
- A pass?

Physical

- Fifty lengths of the pool by the end of term?
- A six minute mile?
- A two hundred pound bench press?

Spiritual

- What are you going to read or study that will help you to become a more worthwhile person? An excellent start is Scott Peck's *The Road Less Traveled* and Stephen Covey's *The Seven Habits of Highly Effective People*. Get involved in yourself beyond passing the next exam. Where better to invest?

Charitable

- What activities will you accomplish this term to help others who are less fortunate than you?
- What campus groups can you involve yourself in?

When you have your goals refined, write them down in the first page of your time daily planner. Tough to do isn't it? What if someone sees your goals?

If people see them, they will respect your organization skills and will wish that they had the goods to write theirs down as well. What if they are never realized? What if you don't have the time to write down your goals? Perhaps they are not yet clear. Take a stab. Demand nothing of yourself and you will receive it.

Whoa. What are you doing reading onto the next paragraph without writing down your goals in the front of your time daily planner? Take five minutes and get it done. OK take an hour, it's worth it. Then you can read on. But be sure to refine them as the months roll on.

Key Event Management Principles

With your goals carefully down in place, you are ready to move on to the challenge of doing all the bits and pieces that you need to do throughout the term in order to reach those goals.

The basic premise is that if you could attain everything that you set out for in those goals, your term would be a success and you would be ecstatic. You'd be happy if you attained only most of them.

To realize these goals, we will need to understand some key principles, or ground rules for success:

1.   Events are the stepping stones to achieving goals. They need to be constantly scrutinized to ensure that they are the right events and that they do, indeed, lead to your chosen goal. Remember that events should include work as well as leisure and recreation items, since they too are important to your overall goals.

2.   Urgency does not necessarily follow from importance. Things can be urgent without being important (like answering the phone) or important without being urgent (like eating enough vegetables). Some things are neither

important nor urgent (I think that housework falls into this category, but that may just be a personal opinion). By keeping a clear line in your mind between urgency and importance, you will be able to properly schedule things and develop an appropriate mental response if you can't get to everything.

3.   Priorities are a way of putting events in their necessary order. "A" level items are critical to your success. "B" level items are important but may be less urgent. "C" items are less critical and have little or no time urgency. You should consider a day successful if you completed all of your A's and got a good start on your B's. What about your C's? Don't sweat them. You are the one that made them a C !

Schedule everything

Take another five minutes and gather all of your course outlines, your class timetable and your time daily planner. Cart the whole works down to your couch, relax in front of the TV and tune in to an old Star Trek rerun. As the crew of the Starship Enterprise explores unknown galaxies and boldly goes where no man has gone before, you will be busy plugging all of your labs, lectures, tutorials, assignment due dates and exams into your daily planner for the entire term.

Naturally, things like exams, lectures and labs and tutorials are all A's since they are both important and urgent. By the time credits roll up the screen, the Klingons will be safely back in control, Lt. Uhura will have a secured supply of dilithium crystals and you will be safely in control of the major events of the term with a secured supply of time. It's all there in black and white.

The next day while you are waiting at student health services to have that suspicious itch in the unmentionable spot checked out, pull out your time daily planner and block out your exercise time slots for the term. Things like exercise sessions should be B's. You can bump them if an A comes along out of nowhere. On the other hand, don't let a C keep you from staying in shape.

I know. You have been booking all of these exercise slots in your daily planner and its boring the hell out of you. But what else would you be doing sitting in the waiting room for all this time? Reading last year's *Time* or *Saturday Night*? Checking out the other patients to guess what they have? Come on, take a moment to schedule in a daily slot to work on specific assignments and to review lecture materials.

What? No time left?

As you schedule in time for lectures, exercise, assignment work and social events, be sure to leave some buffer zones where you will have a chance to smell the roses. You never know when you'll see one worth smelling. Don't get yourself so constrained that you can't spend a moment chatting with a friend or lingering over a frozen yogurt. In fact, it's a good idea to schedule in some informal time so that those time slots don't disappear on you as well.

Pulling the Day Together

The night before

Each night take fifteen minutes to go through your daily planner for the next day.

- Did you get all of today's list done?
- If not, take a moment to determine specific priorities.
- Is it necessary to do it at all?
- Can it live for a week? Schedule it in to an open spot next week.

What do you need to do to prepare for tomorrow? Assemble the books and papers that you will need for the next day and get them ready in your knapsack (OK, you biz students, your briefcase). Do a look-ahead for the next month as well. Have you scheduled time in to work on some upcoming assignments? Are midterm exams approaching?

Don't use a 'To Do' list. Schedule everything into a particular time slot. As soon as it is all committed to paper, you will find a tremendous drop in your anxiety level. There on paper in black and white (or purple, red and green for the A, B and C's) is proof that there really is time to do it all and actually breathe normally.

Through the day

As you proceed through the day, use the blank back pages to jot down ideas as you get them and schedule in any new events or commitments as they occur during the day. Include social and athletic events, a special meeting with the prof, and newly arranged romantic outings.

Check off those items that are completed through the day, including lectures that you attended and exercise regimens that you had the discipline to follow through with. The sense of accomplishment from reaching your goals for the day leads to a tremendous feeling of self worth.

At lunchtime, have a look to see how the day is shaping up:

- Are you on track with your events for the day?
- Has anything happened so far that will need an entry for a subsequent day?
- Is there anything that needs to be done prior to the events of the afternoon?

An ideal time to work in some exercise is after your last class of the day. A fiery game of squash, a couple dozen laps of the pool or an invigorating jog around campus is a great way to clear out your mind and provide yourself with the second wind that you will need to power your way through the evening. You look doubtful. Better re-read Chapter Four.

When you arrive back home, set aside half an hour to

gather and sort your lecture notes and staple the related notes from each lecture together. Before filing them away in their proper resting places, take a minute and read through them for a quick refresher course. If anything is missing or there are sections that you don't understand, check the textbook or make a note in your daily planner to bring it up with a friend the next day at school.

As you go through your notes, watch for work that your professor has assigned. Estimate the time that it will take to complete (best to estimate a bit high) and when it will need to be done. Take a second and schedule it straight into your daily planner. No need to worry about it any more.

And into the evening

With today safely organized, scheduled and reviewed, it's time to take a dinner break before getting tonight's projects completed. Flip to 'Beyond the Care Package' and cook up the selection of your choice. Know what time your dinner break ends, though, otherwise it will stretch to 10:30.

When you have polished off the last morsel, get back to your desk and get at it. But first, do the dishes. You won't be able to concentrate properly knowing that an ugly slimy scrunge is slowly entrenching itself over all of your dishes into that crusty coating that will take hours to remove. Better make that at least a B.

Back to your desk to tackle this evening's assignments. Take a look at what you have recorded in your daily planner for tonight. Which is the most urgent item, the one that will most affect your grades for the year? Tackle it first. If you begin with the task that you would prefer to do, you will drag it out until there is no time left to tackle the one that you needed to do that night.

Always ask yourself the question "Is what I am doing right now the most important thing that I could be doing at this time to help me meet my goals?"

If the answer is no, move on to what you should be doing. Don't do tasks just for the sake of crossing them off the list. There is a priority to most things. Once each day, be sure to look back to the goal section of your time planner to ensure that your chosen goals are staying top-of-mind.

When you have completed your assignment or project work for the night: Cross the items off your list.

- Take a moment to review your goals for the term.
- Were you able to make progress toward all of your goals today?
- What should you add to tomorrow's schedule to get you back on track?

With today all sorted out, clear all of the leftover paper work off your desk. "Organized Grime" (upcoming Chapter Seven) will explain where to put everything, so there's no excuse for not having an orderly desk at the end of the day. You can tell everyone else that 'orderly' does not necessarily mean 'clean'. Orderly means everything is in its place and at least you know where that place is. (Although I hope no one from my office is reading this!)

And thinking of tomorrow

Once again it's time to take a few moments to have a look at tomorrow's schedule:

- Does it prepare you for upcoming assignments?
- Do you have some buffer time scheduled for the unscheduled?
- Time for social events and fun?
- Time to review your notes from the day?
- Time set aside to make some progress on your Scholastic, Physical, Spiritual and Charitable goals?

With everything down in your daily planner, your desk cleared off and today another successful step toward reaching your personal goals, there is nothing to worry about. Relax. Read a novel. Go fishing. Clean the oven.

Making it all Work for You

It's great in theory, but you just don't have the discipline, right?

Take another look. You can afford the daily planner. You surely have half an hour to review your day and plan the next one, right? So get started. Leave room for interruptions. Promise that you will give it your best shot for one month and I think that you will be surprised.

If your concern is that your friends will keep you from sticking to your schedule, give yourself some buffer time so that an impromptu, all night game of euchre or endless gab session won't throw your schedule out for the month.

Best of all, with a schedule as neat and tight as this, odds are pretty slim that "... you will plum forget about a course that you signed up for and forgot to attend all year... with the exam approaching in a half an hour and ... no clue what it is all about... flunking this course will cause you to stay in school for another year and your parents will..."

Relax.

You are in control. Really.

=

Organized Grime

=

Papers, laundry and cupboards

Missing Stuff Scenario #1

You arrive home from school, starving to death. Rummaging through the cupboard you find only one box of Kraft Dinner left. The package was opened, but all of the little noodles seemed to be present and accounted for, so you dumped the whole works into the pot. When everything is boiled and ready to go, you pour in some milk and add the ...Where did the sauce mix go?

Missing Stuff Scenario #2

You had put off doing your part of the cost accounting assignment for far too long.

To appease your panic stricken group, you told them that you were just, uh, putting the finishing touches on it. With the group meeting tomorrow morning at 8:00, it was going to be one busy night. But when you got home your roommate was watching the 49'ers playing the Raiders and you figured that your assignment could hold out for the first half. The NFL led to Wheel of Fortune and then Jeopardy, sucking you in for several extra hours as often happens while one is positioned in front of the addictive Time Vacuum. (Is that why they call it TV?)

By the time Alex had asked the final question under Geography, it was 10:00 PM. You dragged yourself to your desk and shuffled through your papers to find your copy of the assignment outline that the professor handed out in class. It should be with your notes clipboard that ... you left in your locker.

Missing Stuff Scenario #3

Hard to believe, but your graduation day had finally arrived.

You had spent most of the morning celebrating at the beach with the gang and had cut it a little close to get home in time to get changed for the graduation ceremony. While you were excited about finally getting it all over with, the idea of donning the corporate duds was less than appealing.

With your best suit enhancing the lines of your physique, the toothpaste residue still in your mouth, twenty seven minutes until the start of the ceremony, a carload of relatives waiting and dad honking the car horn outside, you tear apart your room in search of your dress shoes.

They aren't there.

It's Not Really Lost – It's Here Somewhere

Let's face it. We all lose stuff from time to time. Enough said. We can all relate to the problem. Before getting to some solutions, let's pause for a moment to better understand the reasons that our essentials go AWOL. Being able to hang on to our stuff is an important pre-requisite to getting organized. (Should this chapter have come before Time Management?)

THE LAWS OF DISAPPEARING ARTICLES

The law of usefulness

Useless things do not get lost.

For a thing to be lost, there must be someone in pursuit of it. It's a bit like the old riddle about a tree falling in the forest. Given that it is a useful thing, odds are it's useful to someone else as well as you and they have taken it. Test this law yourself. When you were a kid, did you ever lose the piano theory lesson that you were supposed to complete? Did that plate of liver ever mysteriously saunter off the dinner table so that you didn't have to eat it? Did you ever misplace that ugly sweater that your Aunt Liddie picked out for you and you never wore? The prosecution rests.

The law of vanishing returns

If someone borrows your stuff, odds are they had a powerful need for it.

Enough for them to do a search of their place to see if they have one. Enough to overcome their natural reluctance to ask you for yours. But now, with yours securely borrowed and in place, allowing them to carry on with their business and save themselves the hassle, cost and aggravation of buying their own and giving you back yours, they just carry on with it. When you need it back it's gone. Who borrowed it? Who knows?

The law of entropy

China vases don't gather up their pieces from the floor, refill themselves with water and carefully rearrange the fresh flowers so gracefully spewing over. Bicycle rims do not take time out to straighten themselves after an encounter with a steep curb. A full beer left on the patio in August will not re-chill itself and seek out fresh bubbles.

And your economics notes will not staple themselves together, sort themselves into chronological order in a file folder, all highlighted in flourescent yellow just before you begin to study for the final.

Getting organized

OK. So now we know what a pain it is to lose stuff and we know how it manages to get away. How do we stow it so that we can find it when we need it, you ask?

First, we need to get some organizing gear. For just a few bucks, you can get everything that you will need to amass all of your school notes, gas bills, stereo warranties, grade reports and term papers.

In fact, we will build you a complete system such that, with only five minutes of organizing time each day, you will be able to locate any relevant piece of paper that you will need to find during the entire school year.

Kraft Dinner sauce mix, assignment outlines or dress shoes? You are on your own.

THOSE DAILY NOTES KEEP PILIN' UP

What are you supposed to do with 'em after you write all of the stuff down? How do you know where one day ends and the next begins? What if you lose the one page that you really need?

Begin by getting yourself one of those plastic clipboards with the flap that closes over the pad of paper. Stock the thing with three hole binder paper at the start of each day. As you go to each class, write the course code at the top of each page as well as the date. Number each page as you go, and be sure to use the back of each page to help keep the planet green.

Next class? Get out a fresh piece of paper and put the new course code at the top. Stow your completed notes, cinched with a paper clip (just to keep them in place for now), in the handy pouch on the left side of the clip board. Simple.

End of Day Logistics

Beauty. Lots of great notes. Put them in order of page numbers and subjects. Staple together each complete day's worth of notes so that you don't lose that one critical page. But where do they go?

In your new filing cabinet.

I know. You don't see yourself as the filing cabinet type. What next, a station wagon and some brown oxfords? Does this mean that in the summer time you will have to wear Bermuda shorts with black ankle socks?

Ya gotta do what ya gotta do. Start with a two drawer and work your way up. Be sure to ask for all the fixin's so that you can use hanging file folders like the real pros. If the clerk at the stationary store indicates a lack of understanding of what you mean by 'you know, a filing cabinet with all the fixins', just show his manager this picture:

She'll get you the right one.

Wondering whether these cabinets are made of platinum? Expensive little suckers aren't they? Too pricey? See if the nice people at the stationary store have any of those cardboard file folder holder boxes. Or you might be able to hunt down a good used metal cabinet. They come in useful in later life when you need to seek out the guarantee for the lawn mower, or your spouse may want to track her clothing bills from the previous year for her annual variance analysis.

While the nice manager is helping you, get a whole whack of file folders and hanging folders to keep everything nice and straight. You may even want to get the coloured file folders so that you can use different coloured ones for different subjects. If you are a real organization buff, pick up a roll of those little file folder stickers as well. What the hell.

When you get home, put the whole works together. As usual, they probably hosed you and you are missing a screw or something. The whole cabinet feels like a piece of junk right? Until the Japanese get into building filing cabinets, there's not much we can do.

Oops. You need a hacksaw to cut the little gizmo that holds the hanging files, or a screwdriver to bolt the whole works together? Check around your place. No luck? See if you can borrow one from a neighbour. Give it back when you are done.

Getting it all together

The top drawer of your filing cabinet is your workhorse.

Set up one hanging file for each subject that you are taking using the little tabs provided (did you forget the tabs?) and then set up file folders for each subject – one for notes, and one for each of term papers, lab notes, textbook notes, assignments, course outlines, old exams or whatever. Put all file folders for each subject into the hanging file that you have set up for it. Now you wish that you had splurged and got the colour-coded files don't you?

Dynamite.

No more lost notes for you. At the end of each day, in go the stapled notes du jour and you are all set. Exam time? Cake. Just grab all the file folders for the subject and the textbook and head off to the library (Remember that the library has no fridge, no TV, no telephone. Nothing to do but study.) Sounds great, you say, but what of that mysterious bottom drawer of the filing cabinet? Ah yes, the bottom drawer...

Bills, various, miscellaneous and sundry papers and that Mysterious Bottom Drawer

Your aunt sent you a great inspirational clipping, this time about your dream of composing jazz. Your picture is in the paper for winning the submarine eating contest. Your new bike lock comes with a warranty. You scribble down a great business idea. A summer employer writes you a letter of recommendation. You clip out a *Bizarro* cartoon.

Where do you file all this stuff? And how come you keep accumulating more of it?

Easy. This is where that mysterious bottom drawer of your filing cabinet fits in. Use the bottom drawer for all these non-school-notes stuff. Begin by setting up your major hanging files:

1. Bills
2. Guarantees
3. Ideas
4. Articles
5. Warranties
6. Memorabilia

For each major category, use a hanging file and for each minor category, use a file folder. For bills, you might set up a hanging file called bills and then have a file folder for each type: electricity, gas, water, etc. Store all the bills in chronological order in each file, so that if you have to refer back, they are easy to find.

Still have some effects that defy a logical filing system? How about some stuff that doesn't deserve a hanging file of its own, but doesn't fit into any of your pre-established sub groups? Pitch it out.

How important can it be if it doesn't fit into a pre-established sub group? If you are in a soft mood, maybe you want to take a moment, define a new sub-group, set up an additional hanging file and file the damn thing! It's a good idea to keep your file development tools (hanging files, tabs, file labels and folders) handy for just this type of emergency.

For non-school stuff, you might try getting yourself one of those plastic accordion files. They are handy to get in and out of, very portable and a whole bunch cheaper than another filing cabinet. Worried about moving day? A filing cabinet's drawers usually lock (or can be sealed with good tape). Not a chance of your muscular friends dropping a cardboard box of notes all over the sidewalk. Prevention is better...

Bills

Have you ever had a bill buried under other paperwork and forgot to pay it? What kind of a stupid question is that? Who hasn't? It was a convenient excuse and worked pretty well until the electric company got wise and plunged your place into darkness, right?

The real question is where do you stash your bills during the time that you receive them and up until you mail them. Yes, I am well aware that you are probably mailing them a couple of weeks after the date you wrote on the cheque to solve your cash flow problem and to try and collect the prompt payment discount. I think that your creditors are probably on to that one as well. Back dating the envelope using the postage meter from Mom's office too, are you? Sly .

When you get bills, rip them open to survey the damage. Get yourself some sort of makeshift IN/OUT tray just like the big shooters have. Stack the bills up on the IN tray in the order that they are due. As new ones come in, slip them into the proper chronological sequence.

Every couple of days, under low lighting and with no one else around, gingerly peek at the top bill to see if it is due yet. Write a cheque as late as you dare, put it in the return envelope with the remittance slip, write the amount paid on your receipt and file it in your Bill Hanging File Main Group in proper chronological order. Toss the completed envelope in your OUT tray for mailing the next day. Keep filing the new bills and mailing the old ones from the top of the pile.

Presto. The lights stay on, the phone rings, the water stays hot and you don't get evicted.

Laundry – This is a Good Spot to Stuff It In

Laundry?

OK, maybe laundry shouldn't fit in here, but it didn't fit into any of the other major sub groups that I had already set up. I have some good tips that shouldn't be wasted and this seemed like a good spot to fit them in. Besides, laundry is like anything else: you get the best results when you are organized.

So you come home late, peel off your clothes to jump into bed and what are you supposed to do with them? The simple thing is to toss your gauchies on the floor and test your jump shot with your socks. This approach is functional, but it probably annoys the hell out of your roommates.

Actually this section is meant also to include those other aspects of laundry, like towels and sheets and stuff. It seems they don't require as frequent attention as the clothing. You will already know that they tumble along with whatever laundry divisions you decide to set up later: coloured and whites or whatever.

Enter the laundry basket. A common spot to squirrel away all of your wayward clothes and stuff until you can help them on their path to the washing machine. If you get yourself a basket that is rigid, you will be able to toss your clothes in from across the room. Then you can lean it against the foot of your bed and slide off the sheets but only when they really need it. This ease of access will make it more likely for you to actually use the thing.

A large cloth bag, on the other hand facilitates toting your dirty duds and other items off to the Laundromat. I will leave this important decision up to you. As a big executive you will one day find that you knock off such weighty decisions almost intuitively, but for now, take your time and get the laundry bag or basket that best suits your needs.

Every school has those nerds who will carefully separate out their whites from their coloureds, using different wash temperatures and detergents for each. These people should be in the washers with their carefully sorted laundry. By the time I graduated, however, I do have to admit that virtually all of my clothes had converged into a single colour. It was kind of a muted purplish-grey, yet another confirmation of the existence of our friend Entropy – warming beer, greying T-shirts and accumulating a mess in the kitchen.

Keepin' the whites white and the colours coloured

The solution, I later learned (from my then-girlfriend, now-wife), is to get two laundry repositories: one for anything close to white and one for darker colours. Take the two containers to the laundromat and wash the loads separately. It was a small concession for a happy marriage.

Reason for separating the stuff is because some colours dissolve a bit in water, whether hot or cold. Today's great detergents – some even contain dry oxygen bleach that brightens everything – don't need hot water. And if you read the detergent labels, you'll not only lower the heating bill, you'll turn the world a notch greener too. Simple as that.

If you are still worried about looking a touch anal retentive with all of this sorting and separating, just take one load to get washed at a time. So you happened to have only white laundry that week. So who's askin' anyway?

I used to have a roommate who had three baskets, one for whites, one for coloureds and one for dry cleaning. I laughed at him up until last year, when I raised him one (small) basket to stow my spare change in. If you have any ideas for a fifth basket, please write and let me know.

Like employing birth control devices every other time, overloading your washer is false economy. Fill the clothes to the top of the vanes on the white thing that sticks up in the middle. Don't use cheap detergent. It's cliché as all get out, but Tide really does seem to get clothes clean.

And what's a wash without a dry?

Do we need to bother with all this softening and anti static stuff for the dryer? Looks a bit wimpy doesn't it? I mean, who isn't strong enough to pull their clothes apart?

Besides, if you turn out the lights while you separate the charged laundry, you can have your own personal lightning storm – kind of a lava lamp for the nineties. On the other hand, how long will it take to live down strolling around on campus with a sock stuck to your back?

Get some of those little sheets for the dryer. The answer to your next question is no, you can't reuse those little sheets or use ones that you found discarded in the Laundromat. The manufacturers are on to that game. Planned obsolescence. But if that bugs you, you might want to try some of those liquid softeners and static reducers. Get your glasses on and read directions.

Organizing the clothes and stuff that ends up as laundry

The sheets and towels are no problem, they just go back on the bed and on the towel racks when they're dry. Right? Yeah, and even if they aren't quite dry. Big deal you say. Now you have gotten your main stuff clean and back where it belongs, and you even got your clothes clean. But how do you stow them so that you don't have to tear your dresser apart just to find a reasonably clean pair of underwear? Hmm.

Begin by noting the number of categories of clothing that you have:

Male students:

1. Pants
2. Shorts
3. Gym clothing
4. Underwear and Socks
5. T-shirts
6. Sweatshirts
7. What-have-you

Female students:

1. Pants and Skirts
2. Shorts and Tights
3. Workout clothes
4. Underwear, Socks and Stockings
5. T-shirts and Shirts
6. Sweatshirts
7. What -have-you plus Miscellaneous

Those of you with less than a seven-drawer dresser may be panic-stricken at this point wondering where you are going to stow all of your clothing. Relax. Start at the top.

The top drawer should be for underwear and socks. Why underwear and socks? I don't know, but they seem to have a natural affinity to each other. How many times have you heard people lump them together? Exactly.

The only problem is that when you store your underwear and socks in the same drawer, they tend to mingle. Sure, it all starts off innocently enough. Maybe a sock meanders over to chat up a pair of underwear. OK, so a brassiere slinks over to borrow a cup of sugar (or whatever it is that a brassiere might borrow from a sock — work with me here). Next thing you know, you have a mess. The socks are out of their pairings, your favourite underwear are hiding up in a corner. It's a jungle.

If you are handy with carpentry, you can build yourself a little divider to keep the socks and underwear apart. Or perhaps you can rig something up out of cardboard. If you are buying a new dresser, look for these drawer dividers as an important feature. Using dividers may begin as just a simple convenience, but they will become a way of life. Refer to the picture below for do-it yourself dividers.

To fold or not to fold?

For the remaining drawers, you may or may not need dividers. In the second drawer, set up your T-shirts on the left and your sweatshirts on the right. By the way, when folding T-shirts you can make them nice and compact by laying them flat on their fronts, folding the little arms and about 3 inches of the sides toward the middle. Then fold the bottom third up toward the top and flip that fold up toward the neck. Neat little square, huh? You should be able to get two piles of them in your drawer now.

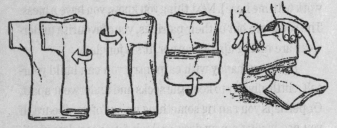

Work your way through your drawers setting them up in this type of a logical manner until you run out of clothes or drawers. My bet is that the leftover clothes are ones that you don't like anyway since most people would put away their favorite clothes first. Give the leftover clothing to charity.

ORGANIZING YOUR CUPBOARDS

Oh yeah. One more thing. How do you organize your food? You could try lining up all the boxes and cans in alphabetical order like they did in *Accidental Tourist*, or....

If you live on your own, you can pretty well jam it in your cupboards any way you can. Try to keep the good stuff tucked in behind the oatmeal, soup and broccoli. Otherwise you will have a great dinner of Oreo's, Sour Cream and Chive crackers and Tin Roof Ice Cream and have to tough it out the rest of the week on a small slab of tofu, a jar of mustard and an eggplant.

If you have a roommate, the dynamics change dramatically. Hide all of the good stuff under your bed. To discourage nibbling from the enemy camp, mark the current levels of your stuff on the outside of the container with an ultraviolet marker. Consider the use of surveillance cameras throughout the kitchen.

Above all go for revenge and vindication with escalating punitive damages. She steals an Oreo, you polish off her ice cream. He eats a couple of your Chipits, wipe out his entire cracker reserves. Somebody gets into your chips, eat their steaks.

As Sean Connery said, "That's the Chicago way."

And here's the shortest summary

Organize your papers, stash notes apart from bills sort your laundry, divide your underwear from your socks and guard your food. You'll make it through.

=

Avoiding Arithmetic Armageddon

=

Breaking the math barrier

It was July 20, 1969 and Apollo 11 was coming in for final approach to the moon. It was to be a day of great international significance, and represented the struggle of a nation to make reality of JFK's vision to get a man on the moon.

In fact the entire mission represented a channeling of some of the world's greatest brain power into one of the most complex challenges ever. The scientists clutched their coffee cups, eyes glued to the myriad banks of whirring tape drives, blinking LEDs, and computer monitors. Every aspect of the flight was carefully monitored and so far everything had performed like a symphony.

Back at Houston in mission control, the atmosphere was tense. Dozens of scientists, astronomers, engineers and mathematicians were staring at computer screens and control panels, completely oblivious to the sweat trickling down their pale tense faces. Their years of calculations were finally being put to the test. No detail had been overlooked, no aspect left unrehearsed, unchecked and re-checked. The symphony of perfection was reaching a crescendo.

Doug Schneeply was a relative newcomer to the Apollo design team. He had been the gold medal winner in his engineering class and NASA's first pick for their entry level training program at the Jet Propulsion Laboratory in Pasadena California.

He had been thrilled to be selected as a team member, but his intensely humble nature had left him feeling inadequate in the midst of what he perceived as the true 'greats' of the scientific community. More than any of the experts in Houston that day, Doug was nervous.

He had repeatedly checked his work and was unable to find any errors. His responsibility within this mission was the control relay system that would position the Lunar Module at the correct height over the moon's surface for Neil Armstrong to make his historic lunar debut.

The ship was minutes away from landing.

While the other scientists were tracking the actual performance of the module, Doug was feverishly checking over some of the details of his calculations:

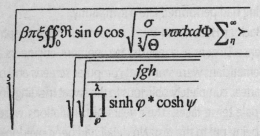

$$\sqrt[5]{\frac{\beta\pi\xi\iint_0 \Re \sin\theta\cos\sqrt{\frac{\sigma}{\sqrt[3]{\Theta}}}\, v\varpi x\!\iota x d\Phi \sum_\eta^\infty \succ}{\sqrt{\displaystyle\prod_\varrho^\lambda \frac{fgh}{\sinh\varphi * \cosh\psi}}}}$$

Suddenly Doug heard the other scientists gasp as the hatch of the module opened too early and Neil Armstrong sailed over 20 feet down to the moon's surface, stubbed his left boot on the edge of a crater and fell on his side, scratching his helmet and shooting up a plume of moon dust.

Neil was OK, but it was a national embarrassment.

Doug felt the furious burning stares of his colleagues. He wished a crater would suddenly engulf him too. Once again he scoured his calculations.

"Oh, no," he realized, it was supposed to be a small step for Neil and a giant leap for mankind....

Millions or Billions, It's All Terrifying

For many people, anything remotely related to math is terrifying.

While much is made of illiteracy as a critical problem, an equally daunting issue is that of inummeracy. A recent survey published in *The Toronto Star* showed that less than half of Canadians surveyed understood the relationship between a million and a billion. A related question highlighted the relevance of this survey to people's understanding of the national debt. If people are that blasé about millions or billions, it is no wonder that our federal finances are in such a state of disarray.

Whether or not you enjoy math, you will find it to be an essential part of whatever you become involved with. In the world of commerce you will need to care about the difference between margin and markup or as a professional chef, you will need to be able to scale recipes up and down. Whatever your ultimate profession or vocation, some solid basic math skills will serve you well.

But I think that you can enjoy math.

To do so, you will need to shift into a different gear. Slow down. Read the problem carefully. No skimming. Work only from logic, one step at a time. Savour the elegance and the precision. Think of numbers as your little buddies. Work on your relationship with them and they will serve you well as trusted companions for a lifetime.

In this chapter, I will focus on some rudimentary elements of math.

You folks getting into Calculus, imaginary numbers, high-end trigonometry probably wouldn't have gotten into it if it wasn't listed on your karma sheet somewhere. You have chosen your path and obviously you require little help with attitude. We will try to work with those who have not chosen math as their central theme in life, and who tend to feel that math is something to be endured, and preferably given a quick detour during a year or two of school. At least, that's how they feel.

Understanding the question

Hopefully the opening story of this chapter provided some important insight into the need to fully understand the problem that you are trying to solve. Most often people fail to get correct answers, because they fail to properly understand the question. There are several reasons for this:

1. They assumed what the question was about.

2. They got bored reading the question.

3. They scanned the question rather than reading it carefully.

4.   They had just done another problem that was 'exactly' like it.

Take the time to fully understand the question. Write down the given information for the question. Assign meaningful variable letters to that which you don't know. Clearly state the problem in terms of your key variables. With all of that in place you are ready to set up your diagram.

Diagrams

All right, so let's get this problem straight. What are they asking you anyway?

You have a woman riding a bicycle that is traveling east at 5 metres per second. Right. Now you say that she is eating a hot dog that is heading into her mouth at 0.002 metres per second in a westerly direction. OK, and you have a glob of mustard dripping off the hot dog toward the ground that is subject to the usual gravitational acceleration of 9.81 metres per second. Okaaaay. Now we have a fly crawling along the hot dog to the east at 0.003 metres per second?

The question is how fast is the fly moving relative to the ground? Yikes! Help. Let me see. Would it be 5-0.002-0.003 or wait, what about the mustard. Maybe if we divide by 9.81. Or does the mustard even matter?

To make your life considerably easier, always begin a math problem with a neat diagram showing all the relevant speeds, forces, masses, accelerations or what have you. I recognize that this is a pretty simple problem, but it could have been much more difficult by including the angular velocity of the pedals and asking whether or not the mustard would have hit her in the knee.

Or what about if we provided the drag coefficient of the fly and the coefficient of friction on his little feet and asked whether he could even hang on at these speeds?

At any rate, a diagram is a powerful tool to help you through virtually any math problem. In fact if you can state a problem very clearly and draw a neat and correct diagram, my bet is that you stand an excellent chance to ultimately get the right answer.

Take a look at the diagram below. By making the speed arrows roughly proportionate to the actual speeds, we can see in an instant that the overall direction must

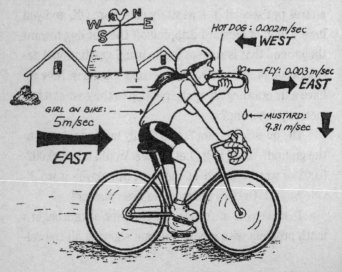

HOT DOG: 0.002 m/sec
← WEST

FLY: 0.003 m/sec
→ EAST

GIRL ON BIKE:
5 m/sec
→ EAST

MUSTARD:
9.81 m/sec
↓

be Easterly. It is also very clear that it will be a number very close to the 5 metres per second of the bicycle since the hot dog speed Vs that of the woman is relatively inconsequential as is the speed of the fly relative to the hot dog. The answer almost falls out of the problem: it is, er, um, well I am sure that you know what it is.

Neatness counts

Having worked in a number of study groups and also as a tutor, I have been privy to the wide range of styles with which people calculate math problems on paper. It matters little whether you keep your room neat. Maybe you enjoy the feeling of walking barefoot in the kitchen with little bits of old potato chips crunching underfoot. That's your business. But when you work through a math problem, keep your page neat.

After a dozen lines of algebra it is incredibly easy to lose:

1. One half of a pair of parentheses.
2. Your mind.
3. A minus sign.
4. Your page.
5. An x or even a y.
6. The meaning of all this.
7. Which numbers were under that cube root sign.
8. A variable.
9. Your patience.

By keeping things neat, you are able to diagnose problems more readily, get help from others, or even get partial marks on things that you hand in.

Word problems

Strange that people with math phobias are most concerned about math problems that are expressed in word format. Hmm.

Well they are really no worse than ones that are expressed in math format. The only real difference is that you have to translate them into math yourself. To solve a word problem, take a deep breath and work through the following steps and you should be in business:

1.   Write out what you know in point form. (The car is traveling at 10 MPH, total time of 2 hours)

2.   Write out what you don't know. (How much distance did the car cover?)

3.   Draw a diagram if the problem is at all confusing.

4.   Look for a formula that you have been given that covers the relevant parameters (i.e. speed X time = distance).

5.   If no one formula has the right variables, try combining a couple of them.

6.   Plug in the unknowns.

7.   Rearrange and simplify.

8.   Presto!

The idea isn't just to get through your courses. If you can become adept at analyzing a word problem and solving it, you will have set yourself up with a superb tool kit to tackle all kinds of problems that will befall you later in life. Or anytime.

Working with percentage

Percentage is just a way of standardizing things as a fraction with the bottom half being 100 instead of whatever else it was before it became 100. For example, 81% is more meaningful to most people than 13/16ths. The SI system is so much easier to work with for the same reason. If you have ever done any sewing or carpentry and had to subtract 8 23/32 from 10 5/8, you know where I am coming from.

The first challenge in percentage is to understand how things change as expressed in percent.

Let's say a stock goes from $6 to $13 (clearly, not any stock that I have ever owned). What percent increase does that represent? Well 13-6=7. And uh, well, 7, and we should divide that by, uh something. Hmm. Should we divide by the 6 or the 13?

The answer is always to divide by the original amount. This makes sense since the question is what percent increase did that represent. The word increase implies a change from where it started. The answer is therefore 7/6 which is 1.1667 or 116.67%. (If you think that is a trivial example, try doing a survey in an office building to see how many working people would get it right. Or better still, try it on your parents just for fun.)

Now, here's the interesting part. Let's say that the stock declined from $13 to $6. What percent decrease is that? 116.67%. Piece of cake. Oops, not so fast.

Slow down. Work logically. The difference between the two is again $13-$6=$7. But this time we divide by 13 since that is where we started. So 7/13 = 0.5385 or 53.85%. Kind of neat. The stock goes from 6 bucks to 13 and you are up 116.67%. Stock drops from 13 back to 6. You are only down 53.85%. Cool. Maybe if you just keep doing that you could make some extra money.

Percentage problems can come in all forms, but the basic principles still apply. Always work through these types of problems one step at a time with no shortcuts. Use less intuition and common sense and more logic and rules.

Get your units working for you

In his book, *Innumeracy, Mathematical Illiteracy and its Consequences,* John Allen Paulos points out an interesting problem: Roughly how fast does human hair grow in miles per hour? Most interesting is that one of his students pointed out as a fallacy that human hair doesn't grow in miles per hour. (If you agree with that one, you will want to sign up for some extra tutoring, pronto.) The rest of you will recognize the need to establish a growth rate and then convert it into the requested units of miles per hour.

Most people doing the calculation will make some errors since it is remarkably easy to multiply rather than divide by a given factor, or to forget a factor entirely. In addition, troubleshooting the answer will be difficult since your page will be a sea of multiplication and division and you will have no idea what you did, 10 minutes after you did it.

To tackle this problem, let's assume that you know that hair grows about 1/2 inch per month. We then need to convert the inches into miles and the months into hours. Since most of us don't know these factors off the top of our heads (sorry about that one) let's solve it using the factors that we do know:

$$= \left(\frac{0.5 \ inches}{month} \right) * \left(\frac{feet}{12 \ inches} \right) * \left(\frac{mile}{5280 \ feet} \right) * \left(\frac{month}{30 \ days} \right) * \left(\frac{day}{24 \ hours} \right)$$

$$= 2.76 * 10^{-7} \ \text{miles per hour}$$

And the great part is that we can go back to the detailed equation that we have developed and check that all the units work out. Canceling any units that appear on the top of one factor and the bottom of another factor, we find that the inches cancel out, as do the feet, months and days. The only units left are miles and hours. Even better, the miles are on the top and the hours are on the bottom, hence miles per hour. Love it.

Since we can easily see that the factors are correct and the units work out, the only place that we could have made an error is in the multiplying. Notice that, if we needed to, we could have flipped the factors upside down. There are 12 inches in a foot, or one foot per 12 inches. Also notice that if we set up the problem, canceled out the units and found that we were left with miles * hours or months/inches or atoms/fortnight, we would have known right away that we were heading for the wrong answer.

Take an extra moment and always right down your units and cancel them out as you build your equation. You'll be glad you did.

The double check

Let's say you wanted to be absolutely sure that the answer you had worked out for a problem was absolutely right. Hey, it happens. Maybe you are writing an exam, you are about to hand in an assignment or a few years have passed and you are working out a debt restructuring proposal for a flailing real estate development company and you would like to be sure that your calculations are correct.

Look for as many ways as you can to confirm the answer. Let's say that you wanted to be sure that your answer for the hair growth problem above is correct. (Why?

I don't really know. Maybe you are about to launch a drive-through haircutting business.) Here are a few ways that you can double check your work:

1.   Check in the book that the problem came from.
On page 9 he says that it is about 10^{-8} miles per hour. OK, so that's a little different than what I got. Maybe his grows slower than mine?

2.   Check for reasonableness.
In this case, we would expect the number to be extremely small and it is. Since miles are longer than inches and months are longer than hours, we would expect all of the conversion factors to make the number a smaller one and they do.

3.   Check the units just like we covered in the last section.

4.   Work the math backwards.
Take your answer and use the factors the opposite way to see if you can arrive at what you started from. (e.g. 0.5 inches per month.)

5.   Is there another formula or method that you can use and try to work it through that way?

6. **Can you solve the problem graphically?**

For vector problems (things with direction and magnitude, like airplanes moving through space at a particular speed) sometimes you can draw a scale diagram and measure off the resultant vector.

7. **Since all of this stuff seems to work, I think that we may have gotten the right answer.**

Kind of seems like math isn't so bad after all. Go figure.

=

The Taming of the Verb

=

Essays and research made easy

A month had passed since the Macbeth essay was due for your English Literature class. While you were usually confident in your work, surprisingly, some doubts now clouded your thinking. The tack that you had taken was unconventional, to say the least, but then your work usually was, well, different.

Bathed in the unflattering glare of the old fluorescent fixtures, your class shuffled in to the lecture hall. You deliberately sauntered in at the end, carefully maintaining your usual look of confidence blended with a carefully rehearsed coolness. Naturally, the rest of the class sized you up as you selected a prime location, deftly finger-combed your hair and slowly settled on your chair. While they seemed to appear unimpressed, you knew that they recognized you with awe as the star of English 102.

Strange that the professor had never openly commented on your stunning prose, your sleuth-like ability to discover hidden Jungian symbolism, your rapier-like wit and your sixth sense at unveiling layers of human emotion and drama so painstakingly laid down by the great writers of the ages past. No matter. Were Keats, Wordsworth and even the great Bard himself appreciated in their day as the classic writers they were to become?

The professor strode to the front of the immense lecture hall, a study in tweeds, oxford cloth shirt, bow tie and brogues. Do they all shop from the same catalogue? There was a moment or two of fumbling in a briefcase that may, however briefly, have harkened to the great Winston Churchill himself.

Retrieving the papers he required, but without another glance at them, the professor squared his shoulders and faced the class. The skin on his face primarily served the pragmatic purpose of retaining in place myriad tiny red blood vessels that might have been the result of one too many tumblers of Scotch. As he prepared to speak, his ruddy face took on one of those thoughtful higher-celestial-plane looks, usually reserved for sniffing orchids or selling Bibles door to door.

He began slowly. "Greatness is difficult to define. In every generation, people seek to express themselves in ways not yet mastered by the previous ages. Some take to poetry, some to the visual arts, others to the strains of the violin, the rage and rhapsody of the piano or the lilting softness of the flute. .."

"Still others," he added, lifting your essay, "turn their attentions to the writing of essays in a fashion so —

Suddenly, a sharp unfamiliar voice intruded.

"That's a book, not a pillow. Library closes in ten minutes."

Huh? The professor, the class, my essay, library, brilliance, closed, oh my God. Watch — 4:50 PM. Sunday. The fifteenth tomorrow and the paper will be due. You sit there, surrounded by a bunker of books on Shakespeare's Macbeth with little accomplished except a three hour snooze.

It is going to be a long night.

The Most Terrifying Rite of Passage

With the possible exceptions of public speaking, exam writing, approaching your parents for more money, asking someone out on a first date, being picked last for a baseball team, going on a job interview, listening to your dentist fire up the drill, being a nine year old having your mother shoveling endless piles of yams into your mouth or getting thrown into a pit full of snakes – writing an essay from scratch is one of the most terrifying rites of passage ever devised.

Thankfully, you are going to walk through that jungle and find a way of taming the snarly, surly essay beast into a babbling brook of literary delight. Take a deep breath and relax. You can do it.

Organizing Your Thoughts

Before leaping in to write an essay, take time to plan it out. You have likely been given a guideline of how long the essay should be, expressed as a number of words or pages. Typewritten work should run about 10 words per line and 25 lines per page, giving about 250 words per double-spaced page. Double-spacing provides ample room for comments, welcome or not.

Planning the content

Given the guideline, or the professor's expectations, the next step is to plan the content. Go back to the assignment carefully and understand exactly what is required for the essay:

- How much depth are they looking for?
- Are there restrictions or suggestions for style and tone?
- Is it a critique of an existing work?
- Is it to be a creative composition of your own?
- What skills is the prof trying to help you develop?

With all that in mind, it's time to make a list of the major topics that you will want to cover in the essay. Let's say that you wanted to write a 3,000 word essay on baboons. That would be about 12 double-spaced, typewritten pages. Through either the details of the assignment or a little common sense, there are probably five major topics that we might want to cover: Life Cycle, Eating Habits, Troop Behaviour, Home Life and Extinction Dangers. Naturally, you will need an introduction and a conclusion and whatever else your professor has insisted on. If you are working on a word processor or a computer, it is best to build your outline right on your system as follows:

1. Introduction
2. Life Cycle
3. Eating Habits
4. Troop Behaviour
5. Home Life
6. Extinction Dangers
7. Conclusion

Break down major topics to simpler sub-topics

Next step is to further break down your topics into simpler sub-topics through the use of appropriate subheadings. Again, use a touch of imagination. Life Cycle is going to include all the steps of any animal's life cycle. While you may not know all the details yet, you can likely make some reasonable assumptions. Add in your sub headings in appropriate groupings and you have built a reasonable

outline of what you will need to research and write about.
Here is a sample:

1. Introduction
2. Life Cycle
   a. Infants
   b. Young Adults
   c. Adults
   d. Mating
   e. Pregnancy
   f. Birth
3. Eating Habits
   a. Consumption Levels
   b. Main Food Groups
   c. Seasonal Differences
4. Troop Behaviour
   a. Bonding
   b. Fighting
   c. Leadership
   d. Mate pairing
   e. Troop Migration
5. Home Life
   a. Shelter
   b. Seasonal Adaptation
   c. Caring for Young
   d. Daily Patterns
6. Extinction Dangers
   a. Poachers
   b. Environment Risks
7. Conclusion

Compare your outline with what was requested in the assignment. If it looks like it fits the bill, you are all set. If not, modify your outline to include all the topics that you should be covering. You may also need to modify your outline as you begin your research. Holy cow! I mean baboon. In under five minutes, you have gone from a blank sheet of paper to a sous-essay . A little game of fill-in the blanks and you are in business.

Another way to build the content outline

Notice that the type of outline that we have structured above may be a little difficult to work with for some people. It has a decidedly analytical (left brain) look with all those headings and sub-headings. For those right brain types out there, you may want to build your outline using an association chart instead.

Begin with a circle on a page and write in the central topic of the theme, in our case, baboons. Draw a line outward from the circle to another circle with any related topic that you can think of. Again the same topics would come to mind: Life Cycle, Eating Habits etc. From these satellite circles, you can in turn branch off to even finer categories.

Although you will likely end up with the same outline, some people find that they can work better this way. When your association chart is done, you can then build an outline on paper or on your computer by making the central circle your title, the satellite circles become your

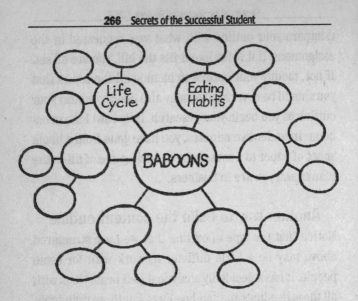

sub headings and your sub-satellite circles become your sub-sub headings.

Now, with 12 double-spaced pages to write and five major topics, you can allocate about two pages per topic, plus one page for an introduction and one for conclusions. If each topic averages four sub points, you can allow about one half page for each. The good news is that half a page in the world of double-spaced typing is really only a paragraph.

It is far easier to think of your essay as a collection of paragraphs than as a 3000 word ordeal.

Filling in the blanks

At last. Time to print off your outline and head to the library armed with writing utensils, a pad of paper and a tuna sandwich. (Eat the sandwich on the way to the library. You will need the fuel.) At the library, you will find all of the information that you need to assemble your 20 paragraphs and get this essay out of your life. All you have to do now is locate the information, get some notes down in point form and pull it all together. This neglects the small problem that you have likely never set foot in a library before. Since the library is an important ally, I will devote a section to it.

The Library. A map may be helpful?

While these buildings are a lot less fun than campus game rooms, pubs or the gym, there will be times when you will actually have to venture into one. Even cool types like you can make occasional use of libraries without destroying – perhaps even enhancing – your image.

To begin, check some of your orientation materials to find a map that will show you how to get to the library. If necessary, take the little map along with you as you go. The library is usually a large and imposing structure beckoning you to the rewards of higher learning. There will likely be an inscription to that effect somewhere in the foyer. In the front of the structure there will be a number of large heavy doors. Pull one open and step inside. Ahh. Lots of books. Also people eating potato chips as quietly as possible. If Dan Quayle is reading this or is perhaps working on an essay, he may want to note the spelling of potato in the last sentence.

Finding what we need:
Compass, Geiger counter or librarian?

How on earth are you going to find your baboon books? There must be a million books in there. There are computers and things to help you, but let's not kid ourselves. Nobody really knows how to use the damn things and the few that do aren't talking. Some computer firm probably got a tax break by donating them. The book that you want probably won't be on the computer and they generally change the floors and racks around every few months just to keep it really challenging

Only the uninitiated or the exceptionally well trained would actually head out looking for a book on their own.

To make life easier, locate one of the librarians. Usually in their thirties, librarians can be recognized by their turtlenecks, corduroy pants and sensible shoes with squishy rubber soles, usually all in earth tones. Sandals with low environmental impact and undyed wool socks are also popular. Female librarians often favour pony tails or frizzy auburn hair. Male librarians favour pony tails or frizzy auburn hair, often adding beards to distinguish themselves from the female librarians. Naturally, coke bottle glasses are de rigueur.

Pick out the librarian of your choice, avoiding any that appear exceptionally busy or those with scowls. Begin your approach as unassumingly as possible. Try some soft-shoe lines like "Gosh, the library is so big, perhaps you can help me..." Salting in words like "gosh" and "gee whiz" will help them relate better to you and if you display sufficient gratitude, they will lead you right to the texts you are looking for. They always get their book.

But not all good research points come from books. Librarians (and computer searches) can guide you to other sources which may be more recent such as journals and magazines, videos and tapes, as well as some that may be older, such as archival maps, diaries, histories and so on. Explain your topic and your purpose. The librarian can help you to make some sound choices in research materials that will help you to produce an A + paper.

Eventually even patient librarians may get fed up with you not looking for your own books. You will either have to rotate librarians or learn to use one of those menacing computers. This could even be another opportunity to meet friends or to start a lovely relationship. Be sure to ask questions from someone who looks as if they really know how to find things.

And getting it down in point form

Having located an array of helpful resources, head off to some quiet nook and begin gathering the information that you require. If your professor requires you to cite references for your work, (it's a good idea to do so) then start by writing down the book title, author's name, date of publication and the publishing company at the top of a page.

Scan the table of contents of the book to get a general feel of what it is all about. Flip to the sections that most closely relate to your prepared outline. Make notes in point form and jot the page reference down beside each note. (This will come in handy if you need to look it up again or for those papers requiring specific page references.) Where laws permit, you may want to make photocopies of lengthy passages to review the material in more depth at home.

In large print beside each point, write the section of your original outline relating to it. Continue through all of your books until you are done. Rather than reading the whole book, make heavy use of the table of contents in the front and the index in the back to find precisely the information that you require.

There is good reason to emphasize "scanning" and taking notes in "point form." By scanning and getting down just the main points, you should be done the library phase in two to three hours. Gather up all of your notes and head back to your word processor or your trusty pen and paper.

Pulling it all together

I am not a big believer in numerous rough drafts. If you have built a good outline and have done your research, you should be able to fill in your outline using the information from your notes to form a fairly solid first draft. You can then go back and tune it up a bit. Keeping all the information in point form for now will automatically keep you focused, rather than getting carried away with verbiage.

Start with the section that interests you most. If any. Move down to the appropriate section in your outline and insert some room under a subheading. Each subheading should be one or two paragraphs. Re-read your notes on this subheading and digest it all in your mind. Are there one or two main themes?

By the way, you computer hackers out there may find it very easy to type in the outlines, then do a cut and paste job to copy the entire outline just below the original. Now here's the nifty part. The first copy of the outline is now your table of contents and the second copy is the one that you will fill in the blanks to form the actual essay. The headings of the outline now become headings within the essay, the table of contents agree perfectly with the content of the essay, the earth continues to revolve around the sun and we inch slowly towards solving the problems of the national debt and world peace. And writing organized essays.

Back Up:
A Bit About the Basics

What is a paragraph?

Get down your thoughts and those of your references, with just one major thought per paragraph. Each paragraph should begin with an introductory sentence outlining the major thought of that paragraph. The real pros call this the Topic Sentence. If you want to nonchalantly toss this term in while chatting with your friends feel free as in the following exchange:

Friend : "Uh, wow man, have you even looked at this essay? Looks like its going to be a real *&^%%$"

You : "Well, having built my Association Chart, set up my Outline and written my TOPIC SENTENCES, I think that I am in pretty good shape."

The next sentence or two should provide additional information that elaborates on the topic sentence. The final sentence should pull together the parts of the paragraph's theme and provide a link to the next paragraph.

Work your way around the outline, filling in paragraphs with ideas from your references and work in your own ideas if you are allowed or encouraged to do so by your professor. When you have filled in all of the blank sections, pull out the original assignment from the professor and highlight her expectations of what information was to be included in the essay.

Are you missing anything important? Go back and dense that section up a bit. Everything seem to be there? Great. Now its time to iron out the punctuation, grammar and spelling problems that are sure to appear. This is an excellent time to get some use out of that dictionary that has been gathering dust in the corner of your room.

Punctuation, grammar and spelling

Ugh. If you were born after 1960, you were educated in a period when reading, 'riting and 'rithmetic took a back seat to learning things that kids wanted to learn; playing with mud pies, finger painting, creative cooking, social dance, badminton or inter-group skills. This experimental phase in early education, however warm and harmonious it may have seemed at the time, has left us with a generation who wouldn't know a subjective completion if they sat on one.

Worse, they didn't build any skills at writing essays. Improving grammar and spelling is not a lot of fun, but it is important. Mistakes in this area can cost a lot of marks. More importantly still, it makes good sense to sort out your writing problems now, before they cost you more than marks in the business or professional world. Luckily, we can isolate some more common errors and correct them.

Common mistake number 1:
Using different tenses

Tenses tell when things happened. Generally in an essay, you should try to keep it all in one tense, usually the present tense, unless the paper is about a historical event. Mixed tenses confuse the reader.

As an example: "Baboons stood about four feet tall and they have thick brown fur over their bodies." The sentence begins in past tense and ends in present tense. To correct this sentence, 'stood' could be changed to 'stand' or 'have' could be changed to 'had,' depending on the tense used in the rest of that paragraph and whether or not baboons still have thick brown fur all over their bodies.

Today of course it would be politically incorrect to show a baboon without clothing, thus exposing his or her thick brown fur. In addition, it would be important not to single out those baboons with thick brown fur for fear of discriminating against the odd albino baboon who could potentially lodge a complaint with the Baboon Rights High Commission.

Common mistake number 2:
Writing in the first person

Huh? The first person? What am I talking about? The first person is a term that simply means you, the writer. Most essays should be written in the third person, or in an impersonal form that leaves the author out of his own work. For example:

"In conclusion, I think that baboons face extinction in the coming decade."

This involves the author in the text of the writing. Leave out the "I's" and the "I thinks" and keep the writing impersonal, unless otherwise instructed in the assignment. Impersonal and "objective" would be like this:

"It may be concluded, that baboons face extinction in the coming decade."

Common mistake number 3:
Word repetition

Try not to use the same word more than once in a sentence or in adjacent sentences. It is not technically a grammatical error, but it detracts from your otherwise fine writing style. As an example:

"Baboons are fairly large creatures and their large size can frighten potential attackers."

A better sentence would be: "Baboons are fairly large creatures and their considerable bulk can frighten potential attackers"

If you find yourself caught with a lot of word repetition, get a copy of *Roget's Thesaurus* and use it to help find the word you need. For the uninitiated, a Thesaurus is a book that helps you to find alternate or better word choices. It is not a *Jurassic Park* sequel. You word processor types can likely access a built-in Thesaurus feature.

Common mistake number 4:
Sound-alike words

There is no easy fix to this one, but a common mistake is to use words that sound exactly like or close to the actual word that you want. Best bet is to get the resident class brain to proofread your essay and then try to learn from the changes that she made. Examples of sound-alike words include: their and there, its and it's, two, to and too, apprised and appraised, practice and practise, insure and ensure, principle and principal, affect and effect etc. If in doubt, look up their exact meaning in your dictionary.

Common mistake number 5:
Possessive forms

I know, more writer's jargon. Occupational hazard. Possessives are simply when someone owns something. For example:

"The baboon's claws...".

In this case the possessive form was correctly used since there was only one baboon. If there are several baboons then we would say, "...the baboons' claws." The form s' is also correct if the being that owns something has a name or title that ends in an s. For example, it is "Gus' Pizza" not "Gus's Pizza". It's all in how you place your apostrophe.

If that isn't confusing enough, consider the word 'its'. 'Its' is actually the possessive form, as in "Who took its dish?" It's is not the possessive form, it simply is the short form of "it is". In summary, check your possessive forms carefully.

Common mistake number 6: Typographical errors

I grow ever more obtuse. 'Typos' are simply typing errors. Often they involve transposing letters to give you words like "teh" rather than "the", "otfen" instead of "often" or "ohme" rather than "home". If your word processor has a spell checker, you can quickly catch most of these types of mistakes. If not, you will have to give it a very careful proofreading. That's a good idea anyway, even after spell checking. Having a friend proof your work is another good idea since a fresh pair of eyes will be more likely to catch your errors.

Common mistake number 7: Run-on sentences

The issue is not the sentence length, rather it is how many thoughts are in it. A sentence must have one complete thought, not twelve. Read your sentences carefully. If they seem awkward or if you need to hyper-ventilate while reading them aloud, it may be time to do some judicious pruning. If it is possible to split a sentence in two, do it. And reading your work aloud is always a good idea.

Example: "A large male baboon approached the troop leader, bared his chest and shrieked so loudly that he could be heard for miles around, summoning other members to step forward, anxious to protect their peers and all that they had worked so hard to build in this vast arid land."

This could be re-written to read more clearly and more effectively:

" A large male baboon approached the troop leader, bared his chest and shrieked loudly. Baboons responded by stepping forward, anxious to protect their peers and all that they had worked so hard for."

Common mistake number 8: Sentences that aren't

A close cousin to the run-on sentence is a sentence that is missing one or more of the things that make it a sentence. Go ahead, help a sentence to be itself. Example: "The largest baboon troop ever." This is not a sentence because there is no verb and no object. More simply put, there is no action word and no receiver of the action. To make it into a sentence, it needs the rest of the complete thought. For example: "The largest baboon troop ever, thundered along the plains, in search of greener pastures."

For emphasis or style, non sentences are sometimes used, but this procedure is not advisable for serious essays. It works in books like this one, though. Right?

Common mistake number 9:
Un-parallel construction

Parallel construction is used when more than one item acts as the object in a sentence. The trick is to use similar wording around both objects. For example: "The baboon shrieked loudly, sending the aggressors to the hills and trees." The correct form would be: "The baboon shrieked loudly, sending the aggressors to the hills and to the trees." Note how the hills and the trees receive similar treatment. This is what is meant by "parallel" construction.

Common mistake number 10:
Punctuation

Here are the most common offenders: When writing out a list of items, separate the items with commas except for the last two items, which should be separated with an 'and' and no commas. For example, "Baboons' eyes frequently signal their interest, their state of health, their sexual state and their age."

A colon (:) is used to preface an example or a list. All sentences begin with a capital letter and end with a period. Days of the week and months of the year, people's names and titles, country and city names and product names are capitalized, virtually everything else isn't.

When using apostrophes, use them where the letters are missing. For example, isn't is a contraction of is not. The apostrophe goes where the letter (the o) is missing, not where the space between the words is missing. Hey, I don't make the rules, I just try to tell you how it is. OK? And for other stuff that may prove confusing, check your bookstore for some paperback versions of style and grammar guides. A big help is Don Le Pan's *The Broadview Book of Common Errors in English,* second edition.

The Finishing Touches: Introduction, Conclusion and Bibliography

No, the introduction is not written first

With the body of your text written, you are ready to add the finishing touches. Write a brief introduction that scopes out your paper and defines what it is that you hoped to accomplish. By writing the introduction last, you will have the body of the essay clearly in your mind and can concisely define the scope of your work. As with the rest of your essay, keep it impersonal. Use: "It is difficult to fully define the lifestyle of the baboon...," rather than: "I will cover only the main areas of baboon lifestyle..."

But the conclusion is written last

Your conclusion section should be brief but should pull together the most important points of the rest of the paper. While the conclusion should not introduce additional factual information, it is an appropriate section to add your own thoughts and solutions to the issues that you have covered.

The conclusion should give your reader a neat summary of the situation and the main points covered. Suggestions for further research could be made, as well as related but differing views and directions.

Bibliography: The sources you did use and others that could be used

If a bibliography is required, you have a little more work ahead of you.

Begin by re-reading the assignment to find out what your professor prefers. There are many style books on footnoting and citing references. One of the simplest and most widely accepted is simply to number all references in the order of presentation within the body of the work with tiny numbers placed above the word or phrase taken from another source. This is called 'sur-numbers,' or 'superscript.'

In the back of your essay devote a separate page to the bibliography and list each numbered reference in the following format:

1. Baldwin, Michael and Grizzly, William, *Baboon Mating Behaviour,* Wild Boar Press, 1989.

Also widely used is the APA system (American Psychological Association) where the author's name, date of publication and page numbers are in brackets following the quote like this: "...through the forests" (Brown, 1987:23). If this system is used, the bibliography will be listed in alphabetical order by author's surname.

Don't get creative in your referencing. Spend some time to understand the style required and carefully check to ensure that your references are properly quoted. Small errors in references are common. Check yours one extra time.

Give the essay to a friend to read over, make your final changes, print it off on decent paper, hand it in early and head off to a part of the campus that you find easier to locate than the library. You deserve it.

=

CHAPTER 10

Making the Grade

=

You too can pass exams

Dawn. Sunlight begins to sneak past your makeshift bedsheet curtains. The soft warm woolliness of your sleepy mind parts slowly, a sense of uneasiness spreads, then fear rushes in.

Instinctively, your head snaps backward trying to focus on the glowing red digits: 6:54 AM. Damn. You had set it for five, giving you a couple of extra hours of study time for today's calculus final. Allowing yourself only seconds to panic, you leap from your bed. The fear that began in your head has trickled down to your stomach. The bathroom mirror highlights the corduroy bedspread marks on your face and confirms what is now obvious – you were up late studying and you have slept in. Lurking behind that harsh visage is a mind incapable of writing an exam.

Your tongue slithers over teeth wearing tiny fuzzy sweaters. You grab for the tube of toothpaste. Empty. Ugh. A swoosh of the plastic curtain, a spin of the knobs and the shower splashes ice water on you. Another unpaid gas bill?

Dried off now and clothed, you sit at your desk, desperately trying to soak up chapters 14 through 23. As your bleary eyes strain at the page, the squiggly symbols and Greek letters of calculus dance together in a passionate Samba. Clearly, it is just not soaking in. If only you had set aside a little more study time earlier...

Forty minutes until the exam starts. You decide to trek up to school, to see if anyone is around to commiserate and to exchange last minute tips.

The cool morning air braces your face and plays with your hair to the familiar sound of your rusty bicycle chain. Your bike follows the route it has taken a hundred times before. With a click, your machine is safely locked to the "No Bicycle Parking" sign. You bolt up the well-worn concrete steps to be greeted by the throbbing masses about to write Calculus 100. Scott stops you, his face screwed up in anguish.

"Get a load of this," he stammers, "Have you tried this problem where you have to differentiate the whole surface of the moment of inertia in the place using D'Eigenvault's theorem in three dimensions?"

You have never seen anything like it in your life.

The panic that had settled in your stomach ventures north to heat up your cheeks and empty your mind of any last trickle of useful information. Your only hope lies in the formulae that you had carefully programmed into your calculator last night.

"Calculus 100, rows 20 through 50", bellows the exam room monitor, "All papers, books and calculators off the desks."

What, no calculators? You were certain that calculators were allowed. You lower your calculator to the floor, dropping with it your last shred of hope to pass, graduate and take over your parent's composting business.

The polite tinkling of pens and rulers is followed by the swooshing of fresh exam papers on to the desks. You sniff yours briefly to check for that peculiar photocopier smell reminiscent of cooked carrots. Check. You begin with what you know, carefully scribing your name and course code on the top of page one.

Turning the first shaking page, you glance at the questions. Your worst suspicions are confirmed.

The apocalypse unfolds.

Blocking the Apocalypse

Avoiding the type of disaster chronicled in the previous scenario is the aim of this chapter.

The key to writing solid exams is the preparation that you have (or should have been) doing all term. The Ghost of Procrastination haunts us all. However, with a little preparation through the term, some nifty studying techniques and the Exam Power Checklist™, (you can not only pass your exams, but turn them into a unique source of novelty and amusement, and ultimately into a hobby that you can enjoy for the rest of your life. Unfortunately, due to space limitations, we will only be able to cover how to pass them.

Preparing a fair schedule

Give yourself a fair schedule. Include ten minute breaks every hour. Use these breaks for a brief exercise period to help keep you alert and ready for the next hour. Try jogging on the spot, push-ups, sit-ups or whatever else you find invigorating. Set a reward for yourself at the end of your study session to motivate you to complete your work on time.

By setting a reasonable schedule and tracking your performance, for example, "I need to complete chapters

28-32 by 10:00 PM," you will be helping yourself to stay on track and ensure that you are accomplishing your priorities. Over time, you will find that you are able to stay on track for progressively longer periods. A half an hour of studying intensely can cover a lot of material.

Attending lectures

One of the grim little facts about passing exams is that you are going to have to attend lectures to be successful. The lecture itself provides some key benefits that are difficult to obtain from any other source:

• You will have an opportunity to see the material in a 'live' format. Is Pearl Jam better on CDs or in concert? OK then, you get my point.

• You will have a unique opportunity to understand what the professor thinks is important. Who sets the exams? Uh huh.

• You will have a chance to ask questions, or even better, listen to the answers of questions that other people ask.

Incidentally, don't let lectures puncture your confidence. Professors have a sadistic little habit of scrawling out four blackboards worth of material and then punctuating their work with a comment such as "Naturally, this portion is merely the trivial underpinnings of a far more significant piece of work which I will attend to presently..."

While you are totally lost, remember that when they

say that, they mean that it is trivial for them, since they have been repeating the stuff to students for the last 25 years. Did the prof understand it the first time he heard it? Fat chance. He wants you to feel as dumb as he did.

Listening actively

Begin by staying awake in class.

Don't spend the entire lecture copying from the board to your notes. The idea is to learn, not to improve your penmanship. By simply copying material onto your paper, you are listening passively while your cerebral cortex is out enjoying a casual round of golf with your medulla oblongata. Get those brain parts working for you!

To listen actively, you must ask yourself questions as you listen to the concepts:

• Does the stuff make sense?

• Do the results seem reasonable?

• Can you relate this information to any familiar situation?

If you have been keeping up with your work and you are still lost, put up your hand and ask for an explanation. Don't burden the rest of the class with infinite niggling details and minutiae, just confine yourself to the one or two biggies that may be driving you crazy. Other people are probably wondering about the same things.

By tuning in to the concepts the first time that you hear them, you are allowing yourself at least one exposure to the material. By asking yourself questions and relating the material to things that you are familiar with, you will be listening actively and you will be helping to motivate yourself to learn the next piece of information.

Helping the concepts to gel: Periodic review

The second opportunity to learn comes during a periodic review of the material. This is best done at the end of each day after classes are over. It needn't take up the entire evening, but aim for at least fifteen minutes of review for each hour of lecture material.

The review period will allow the concepts to gel in your head and also give you an opportunity to find errors in the class notes and work through the sample lecture problems or case studies.

Better to identify errors, omissions or things that don't make sense now, rather than at 11:45 on the night before the exam. Not that you would ever find yourself in that situation. Right?

With minimal effort, you have now seen the course material at least twice. You will also ensure that your class notes are complete and that there existed at least one point in time where you understood it all.

Textbooks are Not Just for Lining the Shelves

Ah yes, they looked so good lined up like shiny cardboard soldiers the day you brought them home from the bookstore and perched them in alphabetical order on your bookshelf. Well, even though they aren't really soldiers, it is now time to get them off the shelf and exercise their little spines. Best not to leave them in their pristine state right up until the end of the term. Or until your parents come to visit, whichever comes first. Speaking of whom, always be sure to eliminate any other clues that you haven't been studying well before the folks —or any family members — arrive.

The course textbook offers another way of visualizing the information because it provides several features:

- It may have a number of worked examples of exam-type problems or scenarios.
- It operates at the pace you set.
- It has fewer errors than your own notes.
- It never comments on your learning ability or tells you that the material is trivial.

Reading actively

So, it's as simple as turning on the stereo, steeping a pot of mellow tea, laying on the couch and gazing at the pages, right? Wrong. The key to learning is reading actively.

Start by sitting at your desk to study. Working at your desk adds an element of gravity to the moment and triggers your subconscious mind to get serious. It can also help you avoid the inevitable distractions of the refrigerator, the TV, the stereo, squeezing zits, chatting with roommates, yapping on the phone, reading the newspaper, falling asleep or waxing the cat.

Arm yourself with a pad of paper and a pencil. Start by reading the objectives of the chapter or the section headings so you are at least familiar with what you are about to learn. Jot these down on your pad together with any questions that spring to mind about the topic.

Try to build up some curiosity about the topic so that you are actively searching for answers as you read. What's that you say, you can't summon up any curiosity about Calculus, Greek Mythology, Meteorology or what ever it is that you are studying? Shame on you.

At any rate, prepare to read. Use a highlighter to draw attention to key concepts, passages or formulae. The idea is not to create a symphony of colour on the page or to minimize the area of the remaining white space. Just go over the key points. Find these elusive little suckers by continuously asking yourself:

What is this about?

What is most important here?

What is the author trying to say?

Be sure to highlight both the material itself as well as any phrases that helped you to understand the material the first time that you read it, since you will want to be certain to review those sections later. These key points are often emphasized in the book or form the opening or core sentences of each paragraph.

As you are using your left hand to highlight, your right hand should be writing down the answers to the questions that you thought up earlier as well as the most critical nuggets of information that you have managed to unearth. You left-handed types may want to reverse the procedure. Practice. Some textbooks have a mind of their own and may want to continuously snap shut on you. This obtuseness may require the work of one hand just to hold the bloody thing open.

Save your notes in the file that you labeled for the course. These notes will prove invaluable later when working on problem solutions and while studying for exams. Their brevity will really save time.

Tuning in and staying focused

You may find that you have difficulty keeping your mind tuned in. All students do. Any type of minor distraction will be transformed into an invitation for a welcome replacement activity. Suddenly, paying bills becomes fiercely important. Is that a dust bunny over there underneath the couch? Better get to it right away. The afternoon soap operas, making a sandwich or the gently understated "ten minute snooze" will all serve to separate you from your work.

The way to stay focused is to size up the total amount of work and then set up a time schedule in which to do it. Like any restrictive program (including dieting and personal financial budgeting), success comes from being realistic.

Promising yourself that you will read the second half of Hamlet in an afternoon is like taking an oath to never eat ice cream or chocolate again. You are destined to break that oath, with the whole program cracking up in a basket of eggs.

Working out problems from the text

By far the best way to learn any type of material is to actually work at it.

Using the book solely as protection should your head strike your desk during the initial stages of counting sheep won't cut it. Whether it's Macbeth, Macalculus or Macsociology, make sure that you have a textbook or a study guide that has some worked-out problems or sample essay questions that will test your knowledge of the material.

It is a safe assumption that the final exam will involve something more taxing than signing an affidavit that you have indeed read the three textbooks.

Don't tell me. Let me guess. Laziness and a strong propensity to kid yourself has led you to discover either that there are answers in the back of the textbook, or that there is some kid in your class that you can call as soon as the problem solving gets a little tough. Right? Resist the temptation. They don't permit conversation and they don't provide cellular phones in the exam room.

As a minimum, do all the questions that the professor assigns. If you have the extra time, do additional problems that have answers in the back of the book. There is no point in doing extra problems with only the author of the book knowing whether you got the right answer. There is one celestial being who would know whether you got the right answer, but with all of the grief going on in the world these days, She probably doesn't have the time to check your work.

Extending the Concepts: Beyond Memorization

Most exams involve questions that extend the concepts that you learned during the term.

Memorizing is not sufficient. If you have been solving math problems in two dimensions, the exam will extend it to three. If your course was on baboon behaviour, the exam questions will want you to extend your newly found knowledge to chimpanzee applications.

Working out problems yourself and struggling with them will help to get your mind in shape for that final exam. Hard Work. There is no substitute.

To help you work on extending your knowledge beyond rote memorization, keep your class notes and your textbook notes handy. If you find that you learn something new while working on the problems, take a minute to add this to your notes so that when you study for the final, you have everything in one place.

Above all, remember to savour the agony of studying like the burn of exercising. It is only the remembered pain of studying that makes your graduation ceremony exciting. There is nothing like the straining effort to understand a fiendishly difficult problem, sketching out a diagram to understand it better and then weaving row after row of elegant mathematics, simplifying, reducing, massaging and then finally arriving at gasp, gasp the flip, flip, flip Answer in the Back of the Book.

Even if you were only close to being right, if you fix your work quickly enough you can lie to yourself and still claim victory. What the hell, no one was watching as you slipped in that extra step. Carpe Diem. Seize the moment. Savour the glory.

Okay. It's true. There are other feelings as satisfying. A three hundred yard, ruler straight drive on a golf course certainly measures up. Then there was the time when you finally found the nerve to approach Mary Sue in the cafeteria. As you neared her cheesecake loveliness, the fumes of violets, mousse and Soft and Dry permeated your nostrils and you stammered out something like an offer of a date. Her purring "Yes!" beat both the golf drive and matching The Answer in the Back of The Book.

Actually, she said maybe. But you told so many friends that she said yes, that you came to believe it yourself. The important thing is that ten years down the road, you will probably hate golf and Mary Sue will have moved to Topeka and married someone called Lance.

But you can always savour the fact that you got The Answer in the Back of the Book.

When the Real Crunch Comes

Studying for exams

The best way to study for an actual exam would be to get a copy of the exam before you go in to write it. This is a risky approach. It will likely get you thrown out of school, relegated to spending the rest of your life drifting aimlessly from soup kitchen to bread line, maybe ending up at a penitentiary, making big rocks into little rocks.

There are better approaches.

Try to obtain copies of old exams from previous years. While it seems almost too good to be true, it is not cheating. Most schools will make copies of these old exams available. If not, check with students who have taken the course before. Take the time to sit down and work your way through some of these old exams. Work through problems, write concise answers to questions, plan and write any short essays required. You will be amazed at the startling contrast between what you thought you knew, and what the old exam proved you didn't know.

Treat it as though it were the real thing, allow yourself the allotted time and work alone. When you are done, make notes of all the sections that you had difficulty with and go back to review the material in the text and in your notes. Compare your results with those of classmates who worked through the exam as well. If you can make it through two or three old exams, you are likely well on the way to being ready for the real thing.

Working in groups

Get a study group together.

The ideal size seems to be a group of three. Larger groups turn into knit-and-chat sessions where all the world's problems get resolved except the course material and a gavel is necessary just to keep the whole thing in order. As a side note, the term "stitch-and-bitch" has taken off from "knit-and-chat" in some circles. If the sandwiches are rancid, it could turn into "pearl and hurl." Use whichever you are more comfortable with.

Back to the best size for the group. Two tends to be too small. It is very likely that problems will arise that neither party can solve. Typically the third person will have the answer and will be able to keep the group moving along. This also provides a compelling reason why it is best to ensure that you are the third person and not the first or the second.

Ideally, the group will involve someone a little brighter than you and someone a little, uh, slower. The 'gifted one' will help the group understand the question. They will also make you sick. The slower member will ask just enough 'dumb questions' to ensure that you really know what you are talking about and keep all three of you guessing who the real dummy is. By the way, if after working in your group for a number of weeks, you can't figure out who the real dummy is, you are.

Always have a good shot at the material yourself before meeting with the group, bringing only those questions that you couldn't work out yourself. It should be each person's responsibility to steer clear of any topics not critical to exam success. Use the group session for clarifying class notes, textbook problems and as a forum to compare the solutions of problems as well as analyses of themes. It is best to have the group meeting in person, since three-way phone conversations discussing Plato's Republic can prove both cumbersome and expensive.

By attacking the course early, the final days before the exam can be used for an overall review. If you finish studying early, be sure to sharpen yourself up for the finals by doing some sample problems or questions a day or two before the exam. There is a definite groove that you will get into for each course and a particular mindset of how to solve the type of questions that are associated with that course. It is important to ensure that you are at the peak of that mind set when exam time arrives.

Exams: Get Set. Go!

Exam day dawns

OK. So you've studied, reviewed and written old exams. You have highlighted, asked questions, made notes, worked alone and in a group, always listened, read and studied actively, and all your friends think that you have become a total loser. You hate me for making you do all of this work.

But are you ready to write the exam? Almost.

Exam writing is an art form. To test your skills, take this simple test:

You stroll into an exam room and you notice someone with a very bad cold, constantly slurping the contents of their mucus laden proboscis. A few rows to the right sits a shapely vision in a mini skirt, high heels, a gorgeous smile and twenty three sterling silver bracelets on her writing arm. Seven rows to her left sits a clean cut 'surfer type' young man who is nervously shaking his right leg up and down, setting up harmonics and rhythms that cause the adjacent three desks to resonate profoundly.

The question: Who should you sit beside?

Even a novice exam writer will recognize the peril of sitting beside the person with the cold since there is some danger of either catching the affliction or being sprayed with the distasteful effluent in the event of an inevitable sneeze. Ah yes, but what of the other two choices? Male students may be tempted by the possibility of family money that lurks behind the silver bracelets, while female students may fall prey to the clean cut 'surfer type.'

The correct answer is not to sit near any of them.

The clinking of those bracelets, the vibrating legs and the nasal slurping all have the same effect: You won't be able to write your exam. Beware of slurpers, tinklers and leg shakers. Find yourself a quiet spot that is equipped with a four-legged desk, ideally all the same length. It may sound like a nit, but the rocking back and forth of an ill-carpentered desk can be a major distraction.

But we jumped ahead. Let's start with the dawning of the exam day.

Getting out of bed

While technological advancements like the modem, the personal computer and the fax machine should have made tele-exam writing possible by now, the concept unfortunately still remains the stuff of fantasies. The plain ugly truth is that you will have to poke your head out from under the blankets on exam day.

To ensure that you do get out of bed, set two or three alarm clocks. I know, I used to have a helluva time getting out of bed. If you are like me, you might want to use an old trick that I found helpful. I call it the 'hostile environment' technique. Place one clock clear across the room with the alarm set to its loudest. Make use of secondary and tertiary alarms set at five minute intervals scattered around the room. When the first one goes off you will leap to your feet to turn it off for fear of waking the entire household.

While you are up, flip on your room lights, clear the curtains and throw open the window. Pull all the covers off the bed and throw them in the closet. Crank up the stereo full blast. You have now created a hostile environment where it is virtually impossible to sleep. The only alternative is to stay out of bed.

One note on the hostile environment technique. On thinking it over, I realize that a big part of the success of the technique depends on the good Canadian climate that sends avalanches of snow through your window if you open it in January. With your blankets in the closet and nothing but your scivvies on, you will definitely be forced to get up.

However, you readers who live in San Antonio may wonder what is so hostile about this system. Having spent some time in Texas, I can picture you lying in a bed with the window open, sipping a Margarita, munching on nachos with salsa and wondering what is going to cause you to get out of bed. For you folks, I don't know what to suggest. Maybe throw a tarantula in your bed or something.

Eating. Something.

If you are smart enough or lucky enough to live with your parents, you will likely have a mother who will have a nice pot of porridge on the stove with one of those crusty scums forming over the surface, three eggs sunny side up, four strips of bacon, a couple pieces of toast, a glass of orange juice, a crab quiche and a nappy of fruit salad. If you can manage to haul that gut of yours up to campus, you will probably have plenty of food energy to make it through the exam.

By the way, try visualizing that crusty scum slowly forming on the oatmeal while you are wrestling with getting out of bed. It may be all the motivation you need to get moving.

If you have a place on your own, an initial reconnaissance of your refrigerator is likely to yield three cans of Bud, one bottle of lemon juice, some curled up pizza with unusual green cheese, some onions growing shoots, half a box of baking soda, a half can of cat food and an old apple that looks like it may have been a prototype for an ancient shrunken head project.

Whatever it is that you have dwelling in there, you will need to assemble some sort of breakfast to maximize the power of your cerebellum (or whatever part of your brain it is that helps you to write your exam). Try to get in some protein (milk, cheese, eggs, peanut butter, yogurt) and some complex carbohydrates (toast, cereal, jam). Don't go crazy on the coffee, too much will have you floating over the exam room, shaking with the jitters or needing to find a washroom at a critical juncture.

If the exam is more than a couple of hours, it's not a bad idea to take a chocolate bar in with you to get some quick energy. The wrapper could also be used to hide some cheat notes, although I hear that the exam room monitors are on to that one.

Getting dressed

Unfortunately the concept of writing exams al fresco has not caught on in Continental North America, and clothing is likely to be mandatory where you will be writing. Give more than a cursory thought to what you will be wearing on exam day. While the Gucci number that you bought down south may be just the thing to attract potential dates, it may not be the thing to wear during exams, especially if it doesn't look good when it gets sweaty.

It is best to use a layered approach, since the heating and cooling systems in exam rooms tend to the polar or the volcanic. Start with a watch so that you will be able to gauge your time as you proceed through the exam. Next, go for a cotton T-shirt and add layers of shirts or sweatshirts to suit. Those of you who live North of the tree line will want extra layers while those from more equatorial climes may opt for tank tops.

Whatever havoc they attempt to wreak with the heating and the A/C, you will be ready. Simply add or remove layers to combat cold sweats, hot flashes and the like.

Most schools will insist on a minimum of one layer at all times.

Go to the washroom

Be certain to visit the washroom prior to an exam, whether you feel a need or not. More than one person has lost points on an exam due to an excessively turgid bladder, me being one of them. When it comes to checking your paper over for those last five marks or racing for a chance to drain your onions, there is no contest.

Making your entrance

Milling around just outside the exam room will be throngs of pulsing, quivering humanity, feeding on each other's insecurity like so many lemmings heading off to sea. Don't be one of them. Avoid the group entirely lest you risk having your psyche and your confidence whipped up like a banana milkshake.

Instead, arrive at school half an hour before the exam and head to a quiet corner somewhere that you can spend a few moments reading over your final set of study notes. With that done, read something inspirational: an old Vince Lombardi locker room speech, a Martin Luther King address or some John Lennon lyrics. Whatever gets you psyched up and motivated. With just enough time to get to the exam room, pack up your gear and head over.

In the Exam Room: Zero Hour Confrontation

Hopefully you haven't already forgotten my advice on how to pick a good spot in the room. The front is better than the back since you are less likely to be distracted by others in the room. If you are in your early twenties like most college and university students, you likely have a set of overactive hormones in place and the spectre of rows of shapely men or women ahead of you (only you know which you prefer and these days one can't make any assumptions) may tap into your concentration.

Neatly organize your desk with ruler, pencils, pens, calculator and spare calculator, as required. Unclasp your watch and lay it on your desk as well.

When the exams are distributed, take a moment to work through the:

Exam Power Checklist™ Part One:

- Ensure that all of the pages are present.
- Take a big breath, inhaling and exhaling deeply and slowly. Calm yourself.
- Read through the entire exam. (The objective here is to assure yourself that you do know how to approach the majority of the questions.)

- Divide the total number of minutes available for the exam by the total number of marks on the paper, giving your the number of minutes that you can spend for each mark of the exam. Multiplying by the number of marks in a given question, you will know the maximum length of time that you can spend on that question.

- Use this marks-per-minute number to check and pace yourself throughout the exam.

(Did the math in this paragraph confuse you? If it did, hopefully you are not a math major. If you are a math major, please help someone who got confused.)

Writing the exam

Begin by picking the one question that you are most certain to do well on. The key to exams is getting the points on the board early. Doing an easy one first will perk up your confidence and ensure that you don't get a zero overall. Most exams are set so that even a total buffoon can get some marks. Do these buffoon questions early, lest you spend most of your precious time on the far-flung esoterica, with no time left for the easy stuff.

There is no reason that you have to tackle the exam in the order given.

To do well, you must follow the three "R's" of exam writing which form the:

Exam Power Checklist™ Part Two:

1. Read the question
2. Read the question and

3. Read the question.

It may sound trite, but few things are as painful as getting no marks for a question that you were capable of completing. Often, a misread question can send you off on a wild goose chase, struggling with a fascinating problem that is much more difficult than the one provided for you on the exam.

Gradually work through the questions, saving the toughest for the end.

As you write your paper, remember that at the other end, there will be a real live person who has to mark the thing. The marker has little incentive to go out of her way to understand your chicken scratch or search through the paper to find your answers. In fact, if you get the marker riled by forcing her to wade through pages of messy, mindless drivel, the effort may be abandoned long before she reaches the nuggets of wisdom that you have so cleverly hidden.

Let's write exams so that the marker will give you the benefit of the doubt. To do so, we will be using the:

Exam Power Checklist™ Part Three:

• Start each question at the top of a new page, with the question number written clearly in large numbers and underlined.

• If it is a technical course, be sure to begin with a crisp diagram and the axes labeled on your graphs.

• Give a concise running commentary of your thought patterns to aid the marker in following your logic.

- If the exam involves essays, use an opening paragraph that lays out an overview or agenda to your response so the marker has some idea where you are headed.

- Be sure to state all of your assumptions as you go, no matter how trivial they may seem.

- Use the back of an exam page to sketch out your thoughts and clarify your thinking. For an essay-type question, quickly create a mini outline. (Remember the baboon example?)

- If the exam is of a type where the questions have a final answer, put it on a line by itself, draw a box around it and don't forget the units it is expressed in.

- Be sure to take a look at your answer after you write it down. Reread the question and check to ensure that it is reasonable.

- Are the units consistent?

- Is there a way to use another solution method to check your answer?

When you have completed the exam, use any and all remaining time to carefully check all of your work a second time. Assume nothing. If you have lots of time left, you may be able to rework most of the problems or spell check your essays. If not, at least check to ensure that all final answers are clearly marked and have their units in place.

If it is one of those %$^&!@ multiple choice exams, be sure that you have transcribed all of the answers to the little computer card that they gave you. Inhumane though it may seem, the computer that marks these things generally shows little mercy and no emotion.

Check again that your name is on the little devil, hand it in and leave. Regardless of how you think you did, it's best to remain stoic amidst your pals. Chances are someone in your group wrote a terrible paper and your boasting will make their life miserable. If it was you who blanked out, remember, nobody wants to hear your whining. The main thing is— you are done.

It's over!

Go out to celebrate and blow off some steam. When you get home, put all of your study notes away and savour the feeling. Oh yes. Don't forget to line up your course text next to the other ones so that they can all look like little soldiers again. This time, like battle-worn little soldiers.

=

CHAPTER 11

Creating A Career

=

Post grad proving ground

Wednesday the 18th.

You had written in your day planner. You had left yourself a note on the fridge. Just to be sure, you had set all your alarm clocks. Your suit – well, pants and borrowed jacket – were neatly laid out on the floor of your bedroom. Just to be on the safe side, you even set the timer on your coffee maker to ensure that a fresh pot would be ready to go for 7:30 in the morning.

Nothing was left to chance. This was the big day.

Nobody, just nobody thought that you would be one of the chosen few to land an interview slot with Zootpick Systems Inc. They were the biggest, hottest Virtual Reality software company around. Their stock had tripled in the past year and their management style was legendary. The salary, the bonuses and the stock options were unbelievable.

The real thrill though, was the thought of being there. The leading edge, the excitement, the challenges. But they only took on the brightest, the best. Let's face it, not just anyone was destined to be a Zootpicker. This was to be your day.

The music, the buzzer, the ringing and the cuckoo. All the alarms had worked. Wait. What was that moaning sound coming from the kitchen. Oh yeah. The coffee maker. Beautiful. Things were clicking nicely. The interview was going to fly by. Wait till they hear about your experience, your marks and the class offices that you had held.

Strengths? Yup, yup. Team player, perfectionist, innovator, style of continuous improvement, sticking to the knitting and all the rest of the headings from that Tom Peters book. Weaknesses? Oh yeah. Let's see. Well, you felt perhaps that you were limited by your somewhat rusty Latin pronunciation and, what was that other one that you thought of? Right. You didn't practice with your Medieval lute trio as often as you should. Heh, heh. They were going to love you.

In the shower you belt out a couple of verses of Bohemian Rhapsody. What the hell, it worked for Wayne and Garth. Quick towel off and let's see what's happening in that mirror. Ohmigod. Oh no. There it was. The mother of all zits. Right on the end of your nose. Ah well, by holding your head down during the interview, maybe they won't see it. On goes the shirt, cinch up the tie. Pants, right. Belt, socks, shoes. 7:50 AM. No problem.

Down in the kitchen you pour a fresh cup of decaf Java and sip away as you nervously re-read the same headline in the paper. Oh no. A drop of coffee landed square in the crotch of your light taupe dress pants. Your only pair. Well, by keeping your jacket buttoned up you could likely cover up the spot.

OK, no problem. 8:03, better catch the bus. Bending over to snatch up your briefcase, it happened. You heard the noise, you felt the vibes. Reaching back with your hand, it is confirmed. Your pants have ripped and your butt is hanging out. No time. Well, you will have to stay facing them in the interview and then, sort of back out of the room at the end. (They might think that you really have a profound understanding of Eastern traditions and right away place you in International Relations.)

As you stand, sardine-like , the bus jostling you back and forth, you take some time to plan your attack. Head down, keep the zit out of view. Jacket buttoned, cover the coffee stain on the crotch. Walk in, back out, use your clipboard to cover your butt. Check.

Wait a minute. Oh no. That little kid that the lady is holding right in front of you is starting to look very sick. Her little mouth opens wide and that terrible retching sound begins. The stench is terrible and your chest is soaked.

Well, maybe if you hold your copy of the Zootpick annual report in front of you?

The Two-Sided Sword of Employment

My bet is that you haven't missed all newspapers, all news broadcasts, or all conversations in the past 2 years. Let's further assume that you haven't been on an exchange program in a foreign country where they don't let any news in or out.

If these assumptions are correct, then you likely don't need me to tell you how difficult it is to find gainful employment upon graduation. The jobless rate for university and college grads is at an all time high, we are in the middle of a jobless recovery, so they tell us, but the recovery will be slow.

But there is another side to the story.

In the midst of this employment disaster, no one has cancelled the career ads in the newspaper. It would seem that there are thousands of employment and search firms listed in the yellow pages of every major city in North America. Career ads, search firms and increasing listings in yellow pages must signify something.

And why, when CEOs are interviewed do they consistently list *getting and keeping good people* as their number one priority? Having interviewed dozens of people myself, I know where they are coming from. It is the rare candidate that shows that all-important mix of skills and attitudes. And if it is still possible for the Bill Gates of the world to move to multi-billionaire-hood, surely there must be a way for every graduating student to land a job, open a successful practice, or start a small business and earn a good living.

It is possible, but it doesn't just happen. It takes some planning, some energy and some creativity. Above all, success requires a can-do spirit and a willingness to persevere at all costs.

What Do You Want To Do?

I am always amused by the number of professional training firms, books, tapes, videos and speakers that focus on the need to set goals. They also put a lot of stock into realizing goals, the power of goals and the benefits of visualizing your goals.

All of this stuff is great, but they often leave out the critical part of how to figure out what your goals are. Most importantly, what do you want to do with your life and where do you want to go from here?

First of all, don't panic.

If you are unsure of what your goals are, you are in very good company. It is almost a fact of life for people between the ages of 15 and 35. Before you reach 15, your parents tell you what to do. It removes much of the mystery. Doing what they tell you is a big drag until later in life when you are faced with the much tougher chore of figuring out what you want to do. Beyond age 35, you are either doing what it is that you want to do, you never will, or you will have stopped worrying about it.

It all goes back to that old saying about how there are those who decide what should happen, those who make things happen and those who ask what happened. At least I think that is how the saying goes.

It is important to do some navel gazing and to try and understand the types of things that you would enjoy doing as a career. Set aside a quiet afternoon and ask yourself some questions. Then write down your own answers:

• What are the greatest accomplishments in my life so far?

• If I have a free afternoon, what kinds of things do I enjoy the most?

• Do I most enjoy working with people, things or ideas?

• Do I prefer expressing myself in words, pictures or symbols?

• Which famous people do I admire the most?

• Which of my parent's friends are in careers that I would enjoy?

• Which courses have I done the best at in school?

• Do I prefer to work indoors or out of doors?

• Do I have any hobbies or interests that could develop into a career?

The answers to these questions should help you recognize a cluster of strengths and interests that may be helpful in pointing towards a career. For a more detailed analysis, I recommend John Nelson Bolles' book, *What Color is Your Parachute?* It is updated every year and has become the all time classic job hunter's manual. Another possible route is to see your career office on campus and see if they can set you up with one of the computer-scored interest tests to help you more clearly define your interests.

Oops. Oh yeah. Sorry. I forgot about the other hand. The other hand is simply that while doing all of this analysis is an excellent idea, there are millions of people who have literally stumbled into excellent careers by a total fluke. The important thing is that they were receptive to possibilities as they came along and didn't restrict themselves to taking over Dad's business or working in landscaping because they always have, or because soul-searching, a test or a book suggested that is what they should do.

Jack Ries and Al Trout wrote an excellent book called *Horse Sense* and it throws a lot of 'common sense' on its ear. They offer numerous examples of people who were immensely successful because they considered options that weren't in their 'five year plan'.

I saw an interview on TV the other day with Pamela Denise Anderson, star of *Baywatch*. She happened to be sitting in the stands at a football game when the TV cameras flashed by her, putting her face on the big screen above the field. The fans went crazy and her multizillion dollar (totally unplanned) career was launched. Naturally, it doesn't hurt that she is gorgeous, but you get my point.

If she was steadfast in her plans to be an accountant (or worse – considering the job market – a lawyer) she might still be scanning the want ads. Keep your mind open to possibilities, ask people about what they do for a living and you may find yourself some surprising and rewarding opportunities.

What Are You Capable of Doing?

Important as it is to define your interests, you will also need to assess your aptitude level in your area of choice. Most of us have dreamed of being a rock star at some point along the line (don't tell me that you have never played any air-guitar), but without the musical talent or the essential great hair, we never made it.

You may want to look at your grades in each of your courses as a starting point, but remember that the bulk of the population works in areas that are very different than what they learned in school. It is worthwhile to assess whether you are stronger in analytical or intuitive skills. Are you good at working with your hands or are you all thumbs? In terms of raw intelligence, it may be worthwhile to ask about taking an IQ or aptitude test at your career department on campus.

With a good understanding of both your interest areas and your aptitudes you are in a position to begin sketching broadly at first, the type of role that might be suitable for you.

What Are Your Career Parameters?

When you make a career decision, it often involves a number of secondary factors that come with the primary career decision.

For example, if you elect to be a professional musician, in addition to the primary fit parameters (interest, training and ability) the role of professional musician also involves such factors as working late and on weekends, a lot of travel, a high degree of income variation from month to month, low job security and, for all but the famous, a low income relative to the population as a whole. It could be that you are willing to accept these secondary factors or it could be that you would like to work as a sound engineer in a recording studio instead, since perhaps it involves less income variation, less travel and more general stability.

As you begin your job search and try to define possible roles, you should consider the other career parameters that come with each of the roles that you are considering. They may or may not affect your decision, but they are excellent factors to ask about as you do your research. Following are some personal factors that you should consider:

- Are you open to frequent out-of town travel?
- What type of income level do you want/need?
- Do you need a steady pay cheque?
- How risk-averse are you?
- Can you work evenings and/or weekends?
- Can you work 50, 60, 70 hour weeks?
- Are you receptive to heavy, dirty or physical work?
- Is public speaking terrifying or exhilarating?
- Do you enjoy or hate meeting new people?
- Would you be comfortable selling to people?
- What levels of stress are you willing to endure?
- What would you trade off between work, family, leisure?

As you research each potential area, you will undoubtedly find that this list of questions will reduce your choices down to a manageable level.

Hot Areas for the Second Millennium

Once you have narrowed down interests, aptitudes and related career parameters, you are ready to explore some options that seem to be a fit. The other consideration still left is whether the world needs any more people doing the role that you have chosen for yourself.

Again, there are two sides to this. On the one hand, to enter a career or profession in which there is a hopeless glut with no likely change forecast for the foreseeable future is very likely to put you on the unemployment list. The world does not need any more wagon wheel makers or Cotton Ginny repair people.

On the other hand, to chase a career simply because you have heard that there is a lot of money in it is a sure route to future boredom or simply a realization that you have chosen a career that holds little interest for you. The money may be great, but the challenge and excitement may be zero. Look for a good synergy between a career that is well suited to you and something that dovetails with common marketplace trends.

Following is my own personal list of areas that will be hot in the 90's and 00's. (Wow! The 00's – I like that)

1. **Computers.** Especially those with skills in rapidly developing new applications using up-to-date technologies.

Computers represent one of the last great sources of sustainable competitive advantage for corporations. In addition, they either have or will creep into virtually every nook and cranny of our lives.

2. **Communications.** As the worlds of telephones, cable, VCR, compact disks, computers and networks fold together, we will end up with some sort of giant electronic bouillabaisse that is going to need a lot of people to figure it out, fix it, teach others, and capitalize on all of the opportunities.

3. **Wellness.** As the population ages and the costs of health care become even more burdensome on the strained Federal purse, people will continue to place additional emphasis on improving their chances of well-being through preventive medicine, diet, exercise, health education, and various forms of preventive treatments, many of which are being invented and tested right now.

4. **Leisure.** As the trend of downshifting continues and people explore ways to operate on less income, freeing more time for family, there is increased interest in all forms of leisure activities. The golf industry, for example, is ideal since it carries appeal across all age groups.

5. **Green Things.** With the tremendous focus on the environment, virtually any business that recycles diapers, makes running shoes out of compost or compost out of running shoes, is likely to thrive.

6. **Kids.** Notice anything different about advertising these days versus the ads you watched five years ago? They all

have kids in them. The baby boomers are having their own baby boom. And just like their parents and their parents before them, they think that they invented the whole process.

7. **Grey Power.** The other big population blip is at the other end of the age spectrum. Housing, leisure and amenities that cater to the elderly is another big growth area.

8. **Consulting.** As the world becomes increasingly complex, there is an increased call for 'experts' to work with organizations to figure out how to compete, reorganize, market, sell, learn, pay, provide benefits, invest money, save money and spend money than ever before. Generally if these 'experts' come from out of town they can command two or three times the fees.

9. **Sales.** Although there is nothing special about selling as a career direction for the 90's or 00's, it is a role that is grossly underrated, especially by university and college grads. In reality, it can offer exceptional income levels (often higher than more recognized professions), some very rewarding challenges and a lot of fun. Any of the areas above will be needing strong professional salespeople to make them happen.

As an afterthought, it is also worthwhile to consider smaller organizations or those with little 'cocktail party appeal'. My point is that when it is time to job hunt, students tend to think solely of the large banks, insurance and computer companies, rather than some of the lesser known, smaller but very dynamic companies that fewer people apply to.

Cocktail party appeal? Everyone seems to want to work at a TV station, in mergers and acquisitions or in real estate. Things that sound good at parties. It is possible that you may have a more rewarding career working with an organization that is less flashy. Perhaps there is a recycling company that could use your skills, or a distributor of plumbing fittings or a shelter for the homeless. Consider all options as you do your search, not just the most obvious ones.

Sorry, one more afterthought. It is interesting to note that many of the 'old standby' professions of our parent's era no longer guarantee the continuous employment, wealth and security that they did in the good old days. Today there tends to be a glut of doctors, dentists, accountants and engineers. Curiously enrollments for computer science programs are waning at a time when demand for graduates is at an all time high.

Entrepreneurial Options

Maybe no one ever did get rich working for someone else. On the other hand maybe no one lost their shirt either. Whatever the case, a growing number of people are coming to the realization that the only job security that they are likely to encounter these days is that which they create for themselves. In addition, statistics seem to show that the majority of new jobs are generated by small business or self employment.

In considering the option of running your own business it is important to realize some of the tradeoffs:

Pros	Cons
High potential income	High variability of income
Pride, challenge, exhilaration	(Often) high stress levels
No demanding boss	Long hours driven by you as the boss
No restriction on vacations	No vacations
No annoying coworkers	No coworkers

Be sure to talk to people who have started and run their own businesses. Try to build a sense of whether their personality profile is similar to yours. Do you get overly stressed out when you are low on money? Are you a procrastinator or a self starter? Are you comfortable on your own, or do you like the support of others, especially to bounce ideas around? All of these questions will help you to determine whether you have the stuff to start and run your own business.

A major misconception about starting your own business is that you need to have a great idea. With the great idea, the legend goes, the business will take care of itself and the millions will simply roll in the door.

The reality is that the most successful businesses take a mundane, worn out idea but excel at the execution of that idea. Making hamburgers, delivering parcels or selling hard goods are hardly zippy, exciting or new ideas. But McDonalds, Federal Express and Walmart have each moved to legendary status by building organizations that were the very best at what they do.

Creating Your Personal Job-Hunting Road Map

We've already worked on some of the key underpinnings for successful job hunting. By now you should be able to build a comprehensive master list of industries or institutions and roles that would suit you.

Next step is to do some additional research to find out what opportunities exist for you to either work in or start a business in one of your chosen fields. Since there are numerous excellent reference books on starting a small business (check out the business section of any bookstore or library), I will focus this section on how to target organizations, uncover opportunities, assess fit and land a job.

The first step:
Tell everyone you're looking for a job

Tell parents, professors, friends, former employers, relatives, and whomever else you can think of. Most jobs are gotten through word of mouth or contacts. Advertisement response is a much less likely bet. You can try the on-campus recruiting route or try sending resumes to personnel departments of major companies, but don't hold your breath waiting for results.

The second step:
Do some serious digging

Those same tried and true routes are being worked over by thousands of other grads. A better approach is to do a detailed search process, beginning with some direct research.

With your list of industries and roles, do a trip to the library to find out more about which organizations are the leaders in each of your chosen fields. Get the librarian to help you (if you forgot how to do that, go back and reread The Taming of the Verb, Chapter Nine).

In addition to hunting through Top 500 lists, also consider some smaller organizations. For example, in the world of advertising, there have been a number of cases recently where some brassy, young upstart ad agencies have stripped major accounts from some of the old standby firms. A CD-ROM search is an excellent way to scan the business or trade press for articles on who the outstanding firms are.

Another possibility is to consider firms that get little or no press, or those that are 'also-rans' in their industry. Maybe they could use your help. A well spent few hours at the library will yield a number of firms in each of the fields that you are considering.

If the firms are publicly traded (listed on the stock market), you should be able to call them up, ask for the public relations department and have them mail you an information kit on their company, including an annual report if they have one.

The third step:
Making sense of what you dug up

With these calls made, you can now relax, work on your course work or do whatever it is that you do when you aren't researching companies. In a few days, your mailbox will be laden with all that you ever wanted to know about these firms. Use what you learned, should have learned, or what a friend learned in finance class and shared with you over herbal teas and bran cookies.

From all of this you should be able to digest all the numbers in the annual reports and figure out how the company is doing. The text of the report near the beginning will give you an idea of what they do and what initiatives are underway or have been recently completed. The back of the report will give you an idea about all of the branches and divisions and where they are all located.

The fourth step:
Summon up all your guts and
make some calls

Next step is to call into these organizations to people who are either performing the role that you want, or those that manage the people that do what you want to do.

Muster up the guts to call them and tell the switchboard receptionist that you would like to speak with someone in _____ (where _____ is the area that you would like to work). If they try to put you through to personnel, explain that you first would like to speak with someone in _____. Be polite but persistent. Receptionists have a lot of valuable information, so be nice.

When you finally reach your desired contact, explain that you are a student who is potentially interested in doing what they do, and ask for a half hour of their time to come out and talk to them about their careers. They will usually be flattered by the call and pleased to help you.

The fifth step:
Zeroing in on the real stuff

Through these conversations you will start to zero in on your real likes and dislikes and get an idea of which organizations interest you. The neat thing is that they will also be checking you out and assessing your suitability to their organization.

Don't be surprised if these chats lead to interviews and even offers. Be sure to come prepared with questions and strive for a good mix of questions about them as individuals, their firm, the industry in general and your own goals and aspirations. At the end, ask for some feedback on whether they would see you as a fit and (if you like what you see) what the hiring process is at their firm.

Continue on this process through all of the firms that you had researched and you should be well on your way.

Resumes: To Do or Not To Do, and How To

Sooner or later, someone will want you to produce a resume. Yeah, I know. Given a choice between poking needles in your eyes and doing up a resume ... No luck, you are going to need one. Don't take the cheap route and have one done at one of those specialty places. Good interviewers can spot the mass-produced design a mile away.

It is also important to get across some of your own personal character. Only you know you. By the way, don't look at a resume as the complete solution to a job hunt. People who send out 500 resumes and then complain at their lack of offers, have chosen and created their own destiny. Would they expect that buying 500 pairs of tennis shoes would get them a spot at Wimbleton? Unsolicited resumes, especially those with no covering letters and a couple of typos, not only don't help to land jobs, but they also contribute to the nation's landfill problems.

Use a resume only in conjunction with research, interviews and follow-up calls.

There are dozens of books detailing how to create effective resumes and cover letters, so let's just look at some key points that you can use as a final check on your work:

1. Triple check it for typos, spelling, grammar. Have at least two other people read it over and don't forget to use the spell checker on your word processor.

2. Make sure that the cover letter highlights how your experience relates to the position that you are applying for and focuses on their needs, not yours.

3. Include an Objective Statement that tells the reader what you are looking for. Make sure that it is consistent with the position that you are applying for.

4. Make sure that your previous job descriptions are achievement oriented, rather than task oriented. Help the employer picture the results that you have provided and can provide .

5. Include the month and year of each of your last positions, so they can follow the continuity.

6. Keep it brief. Two pages is more than sufficient if you are just graduating and have little or no previous full time work experience.

7. Add an Interests and Accomplishment section at the bottom. If you are a swimmer, ran a 3:30 Marathon, won a piano recital or spent your weekends working with disabled kids, put it down. Employers like people who are well rounded and accomplishment oriented.

8. Use the writing tips in the Taming of the Verb chapter. One thought per paragraph in the cover letter, consistent use of tenses and all the rest of that grammar stuff.

Intercepting Interviewing Insomnia

So things went well during your casual chats. Maybe your Mom's pal has a friend who is willing to consider you for a role. Or, by some miracle, you got chosen over one of the other 10,000 grads through an on-campus recruiting program.

At any rate, you have managed to line yourself up an interview. Great. Superb. What the hell do you do?

Although it may carry a negative twang, let me begin with a David Letterman style: top ten things that people do wrong in an interview. If you can do the opposite of what is on this list, you are probably destined to join the ranks of the happily employed:

Top Ten Don'ts for interviews

1. Don't experiment with New Age clothing, jewelry, hair beads, facial hardware, alternative neckwear, overpowering perfumes or aftershave, exposed cleavage or chest hair or far-out colour schemes.

Do yourself a favour: don't dress to be remembered.

Err on the side of conservative. It is rare that a company didn't hire someone because they dressed too conservatively.

2. Don't skimp on personal hygiene. As a rule of thumb, employers will shy away from candidates with spinach on their teeth, those who are conscientious objectors to soap or showers, or those who would be ideal candidates for oil exploration programs on their scalp.

3. Don't neglect to ask questions. Someone who doesn't ask questions appears disinterested in the organization. In addition, it calls into question their ability to conduct research, and their thoroughness in making one of the most important decisions in their life.

4. Don't neglect soliciting feedback on what the interviewer thinks of you. With no feedback, you have no idea how to improve for the next interview. You also may appear smug and unreceptive to input from others.

5. Don't forget to ask how to move things forward from here. If you neglect to build an action plan to get the job, how action oriented are you likely to be when you are in the role?

6. Don't carry a me-first attitude. You are on the interview to understand what the company is doing, what they could use help on and to show them how your skills fit what they need. If your sole questions relate to salary, benefits, vacation and work hours, you are not helping them to see your value to their organization.

7. Don't shut down your ears. Listen. Employers want to tell you what they are looking for and are trying to assess whether you are the person to help them. If you don't listen and probe to find out what is important to them, your odds on landing the job are minuscule.

8. Don't spray blame around. The last thing that any employer wants to hear is a whining session. Candidates who moan about their previous employers, coworkers, parents and professors who have short changed them throughout their lives are not terribly appealing as employees. Their complaints say more about them that they do the people that they are complaining about.

9. Don't speak of events, talk about results. Great that you worked like the dickens on your past summer job. What results did you obtain? What benefits did the organization gain? How much? By when?

10. Don't ramble. Respond to questions with well thought out 30-60 second answers. Offer more detail if the interviewer is interested.

Practice, practice, practice is the best preparation

One of the best ways to prepare for an interview is to practice. Role playing is a superb way to prepare for interviews, reduce your nervousness and ensure that you will do well. Ask a friend (ideally a friend of your parents, or someone who interviews people regularly in their job) to role play an interview with you.

Provide them with a one page description of the name and title of the person that they will be role playing, a description of their company and a list of common interviewing questions to use. (Or let them use their own questions). Following are some very typical interviewing questions:

1. What are your greatest strengths?

2. What are your greatest weaknesses?

3. Why do you want this job?

4. Tell me about yourself.

5. What is your greatest accomplishment?

6. Why should we hire you?

7. Why did you leave your job at _____?

8. How did you feel about your marks in school?

What is that you say? Your first role play was a disaster? Great! Just think, that could have been an actual interview. Ouch! Now, I bet that you are glad that you did the role play. Thought so.

Most important thing is that you take it from the top and continue to practice until you are absolutely bored stiff and you are knocking off the answers to the questions like a real pro. Practice everything in your role play: have the 'interviewer' walk out to the 'lobby' and walk you back to his 'office', shake hands, sit down on either side of a desk etc.

When you actually go in for a real interview it will be a piece of cake. How could you possibly be nervous over something that you have already done a dozen times? You'll do great.

Stop reading and get out there. They need you.

AFTER WORDS

This isn't the end, it's just a transition.

The challenges that you face as a student will metamorphose into a new set of challenges that you will face in your post-graduation days.

Maybe your cheque book register will contain an extra zero, but that won't make balancing it any easier. And yeah, you will likely get rid of exams, but they will get replaced by stand-up presentations in your job. The creativity that you used to amuse your blind date will later be applied to amusing your kids.

The tough part is that life is an endless upward ramp of effort.

The great part is that this long and endless upward ramp can offer boundless opportunity for success and personal growth. And the steeper the ramp and the more effort you pour into the climb, the greater your sense of satisfaction and the more exhilarating the view below.

My bet is that however tough your school program is, you will make it through. And although your school war stories will bore the hell out of your kids one day, your old school buddies will probably always love to hear them. And by putting the right brand of effort and dedication, the thrill of your graduation day is one that you can continuously recreate throughout your lifetime.

Go get 'em.

Gord Stein

KRAFT DINNER*
Great Food on the Go!

Okay, so you've got 3 overdue Shakespeare essays, a calculus exam to study for, your place is a mess and your parents are arriving in 2 hours –

Still tons of time to enjoy your favourite KRAFT DINNER, 7 minutes to cook, 3 minutes to eat.

Whoa! Maybe that leaves you enough time to mop the floor and get your underwear off the fridge. WAIT. Is this a noodle I see before me?

For Info & Recipes 1-800-268-1775

*Registered trademark of Kraft G̶e̶n̶e̶r̶a̶l̶ F̶o̶o̶d̶